BIBLE STUDY

I do HARD THINGS

PHILIPPIANS 4:13

HAVILAH CUNNINGTON

HAVILAH CUNNINGTON

I always knew God had a plan for other's lives, but never felt God could use me. I struggled with learning disabilities throughout my school years, which always caused me to have great insecurity about my value and worth. It wasn't until the age of 17, as I was sitting in a car with friends on my way to a party, when I heard the voice of God speak to my heart, "There is more to life than this! I have called you. Come follow me." I spoke out that moment, telling those in the car that I had a call on my life and they were welcome to come with me, but I was going to serve God. I remember walking into my dark house, kneeling by my bed, and saying these simple words, "God, I'm not much. I'm young, I'm a girl with no special gifting, but if You can use anyone, You can use me." Now, thinking back to that day, it makes me laugh how I'd hoped the heavens would have opened up, with angels descending and ascending on a heavenly ladder. It didn't happen. But I didn't need it. God heard my cry and was at work to accomplish His perfect will in my life.

By 19, my twin sister, Deborah, and I were traveling all over California preaching, teaching, and singing at any place that would have us. By 21, we had been in seven different states and Mexico teaching about Jesus and His great plan for this generation.

3

Now at 35, I've been in full-time ministry for 17 years. My husband, Ben, and I are Directors of Moral Revolution at Bethel Church in Redding, CA. In 2010, we started "Living the Good Life Now Ministries," and travel throughout the year speaking at conferences, churches, and retreats. We also have four young sons, Judah, Hudson, Grayson and Beckham, whom we love raising...while making frequent trips to the train museum!

I believe today is the Church's finest hour...if we choose to live with passion, purpose and walk in power. I'm passionate about seeing individuals encountering God in a real way and seek to blow the lid off common misconceptions, personal limitations, and powerless living so others can become who God has designed them to be.

For more information please visit www.havilahcunnington.com

TABLE OF CONTENTS

WEEK ONE   I DO HARD THINGS

Pain has a voice. It says, "Do whatever it takes to get me out of this right now!" It cries to make it stop! All of us choose different ways to respond to this thing called "pain" but what joins us universally is the reality that we are all trying to get as far away from PAIN as possible.

> ***"Pain is not in heaven and it's not in our human ecosystem."***

HARD THINGS happen to each of us. The Bible says it rains on the just and the unjust. This means none of us are pain resistant. Pain eventually seeps into each of our lives. But what we don't think about is the fact that we were never created to handle pain. Pain is a result of our fallen human race. We were never equipped to deal with this thing called pain. It's foreign. It's not in Heaven and it's not in our human ecosystem. As a result, it takes great understanding of how and when we actually began to experience pain and, ultimately, how to release it from our lives.

As children, many of us experienced circumstances that were completely out of our control, causing serious pain. We were naive to the harsh reality that pain existed. At an early age, we learned to deal with our pain the best we knew how. We made every attempt possible to stop it. It worked for us because we were kids. We lacked control over our environment. Depending on how hurtful our childhood was, we developed deep patterns, more habits, more ways to survive in our pit of pain.

Getting older doesn't guarantee we get wiser. Going through hard things becomes a way of survival creating an emotionless experience. We might say something like this: "Getting the pain to stop as soon as possible is a matter of doing   (just fill in the blank)"! It becomes a matter of technique. How quickly can we stop our pain without stopping the flow of our daily lives? "Doing whatever it takes" becomes our goal. Each of us attempt to keep the pain out... *or so we think*. The lie is this: we believe we can control our pain. We believe that pain, as long as it's not affecting us, doesn't still hurt us. This is a lie! Pain is a pit and the only way out is to climb out. If a prisoner feels momentary freedom, they attempt to avoid the harsh reality that they are not free. Pain can render us powerless to face life.

Read Genesis 37:12-24

Think about this for a moment.

Joseph was a unique young man. He was a dreamer. You can sense his innocence in the passage above. Suddenly, without warning and without reason, he is thrust into a pit. This dark, damp place, surrounded by walls. Joseph doesn't have a way out. He's trapped, without help, in a pit.

Many times we have experiences like Joseph. Without warning, we are thrust into deep emotional pits. Places of pain. Moments, so painful, we completely lose ourselves. We can feel entirely helpless to the idea of climbing out of our pit of pain. Each of us would like to know how to get out but rarely do we feel compelled to actually claw our way out. The thought of one more failure may be more than we can bear. So, we merely survive. We lay low and look for ways to function without really living.

It's not hard to fall into pits of pain, but--do we know how to get out of them and, more importantly, stay out?

Momentarily, our pain can stop. We develop mentalities: living in denial, continually victimized, the power driven survivor. We become the "Why Me?" person. *(All of these mentalities we will explore this week.)* As long as we are going around our pain and not climbing out of it, we are trapped into continually believing we are free, only to realize we've fallen back in to the old pattern. Each time this happens, we lose confidence that we have what it takes to get out of our pit.

Consider this: the moment you know how to get out of the pit, you have confidence. Fear goes away. It leaves because you know that if and when you fall into a pit again, you know how to get out. It doesn't leave you helpless and powerless but rather powerful and free. We are not bound by 'what if' fears any longer. You'll know exactly how you got out and what to do if you get stuck again.

Take a moment and reflect upon the pit of pain you've lived in. Was there a time when you were innocently thrown into a place of feeling powerless and helpless? You experienced pain, but had no idea how to get out of it?

You are not alone. You were made for HARD THINGS. The Holy Spirit desperately wants to get you out of your pit. He wants to build confidence through perseverance.

Can you get out of your pit? Yes! Is it going to take all you've got? Yes. Is it ok to be angry? (Ephesians 4:26) Yes, in fact you need to be. You need to feel the emotion of a prisoner. That feeling will motivate you to get out and stay out. Until you can look back and see how dark a pit you lived in and never want to go back again, you are not fully free.

CONFESS IT

Lord, I confess it's hard to know how to get out of my pit and have confidence that I can. I'm going to trust You in the process. I'm beginning to believe You have my very best interest in mind and Your intentions are to set me free. Through perseverance, I'm going to understand what it means to have full confidence in You. Help me to identify the places where I've merely accepted my pain. Pain, I'm not afraid of you, and I will not allow you to dictate my life. Healing is my portion.

I confess this, in Jesus' Name! Amen.

PRAY IT

Lord, there are areas of my life that I have been like a Joseph. I understand that there have been things done to me that have been out of my control and it's caused serious pain in my heart. I realize I have not always been able to climb out of my pit of pain and I have used false comforts to momentarily ease my pain. I ask you to give me grace to understand the full depth of my pain. Help me not to punish myself for being hurt or broken. Let me give myself permission to climb out of this pit and be the full person I'm called to be. Jesus, I ask You to empower me to do Your will!

I pray this, in Jesus' name! Amen.

DAY TWO – *VICTIM MENTALITY*

Before we begin, let's take a little test[1]! *(Circle True or False)*

1. My first response to a setback to is blame someone else for what's happened. T / F

2. No matter what I do, things are not really going to change for me. T / F

3. I often find myself beginning thoughts with phrases like, "I can't...," "I'm not good at...," "I've never been able to...." T / F

4. When things go wrong, I tend to beat myself up. T / F

5. When bad things happen, they are because I mess up. T / F

6. When I'm angry I rarely begin sentences with "I". T / F

7. Conversations with friends often begin with how hard my life is. T / F

8. When friends offer advice, I usually counter it with a "Yes, but..." since they can't know how difficult my situation really is. T / F

9. I spend a fair amount of time thinking about past failures and mistakes. T / F

10. Other people usually cause me to feel the way I do. T / F

---

[1] http://www.findlayassociates.com/quizzes_victimmentaltity.asp

There is a HUGE difference between a VICTIM and a SURVIVOR.

According to the dictionary, a VICTIM is *a person who suffers from a destructive or injurious action or agency.*[2] He or she is someone who is completely subject to the environment around them. They have little to no control over their circumstances. When hard things occur, they happen "to" them and always comes "at" them. A victims only defense is to prepare and act accordingly.

There is a man in the Bible that depicts this mentality to a T.

Read John 5:1-14

Ok, let's do some studying...look at verse 5 and underline how many years he had been waiting there. How many?_____.

Next, write down what Jesus said to the man in verse 6. Jesus asked,

"_____."

Why would Jesus ask this? Don't you think the answer was pretty obvious?

I would suggest Jesus was trying to empower the man. But He couldn't empower him unless he truly understood what was holding him back. He didn't

---

[2] http://dictionary.reference.com

want to just heal him and have him go away rejoicing over what had happened. He needed him to understand his own role. He needed him to take personal responsibility.

How do we know the man may have had a victim mentality? Read verse 7. What does the man say? Write it here:

_____

_____

_____.

"You can ether be dragged along through your hard things or you can just DO them!"

Now, take a moment, dig deep, and answer the next question as honestly as possible.

When you think about changing and growing in God, what is your biggest obstacle?

_____

_____

_____

_____

_____

_____.

Look at your response and if you wrote down anything other than taking personal responsibility, you may be struggling with a serious victim mentality.

The reason I use the word 'serious' is because I believe it is just that...SERIOUS. I wholeheartedly believe God wants to move and act in your life in such a way that anything that is holding you back will be rendered powerless next to the power of Jesus. However, in order for that to happen, you need to get your 'power' back.... even in the midst of this "HARD THING." The first step is understanding that God didn't send His only son to die on the cross for you so you would live bound to a circumstance or person. Like I said before, " You can either be dragged along through your hard things or you can just DO THEM!"

Look at this story from another perspective. What if God wanted to empower the man at that very moment to get his eyes off his own lack and on to Jesus? Maybe Jesus wanted to smack him with the "I CAN DO ANYTHING" message? In fact, Jesus used the man's own actions to empower him. Think about it!

What did Jesus ask the man to do (in vs 8)?

_____

_____

_____

_____.

Once Jesus commanded it, what happened (vs 9)?

_____

_____.

Did you see it? I hope you did! When Jesus asked the man *'if he wanted it,'* He was asking him to get his power back and once the man understood that he was not powerless to receive a miracle, HE GOT HIS MIRACLE!

Take a moment and let God speak to you. What area in your life are you feeling powerless? As you think about it, listen to God's quiet voice.

What question is God asking you right now? Write whatever comes to your heart.

_____

_____

_____

_____

Now, what is the very next step He is asking you to take?

_____

_____

Today is the day to get the VICTIM MENTALITY out of your spiritual life and begin to walk in power! It may be the moment that leads to your miracle.

CONFESS IT

I confess I am not a victim! I may have been victimized and taught to survive the circumstances of my life, but I am going to change. I am empowered to be what I'm called to be. I'm no longer living in a pit of pain and no longer giving into the lies of the enemy. I'm going to climb out even if it takes everything I've got. I'm going to learn new things. I'm going to do it afraid! I declare greater is He that is in me than he that is in the world and it's time to start acting like it!

I declare this in Jesus' Name! Amen.

PRAY IT

Lord, I asked you for grace to do your will today. I understand that you're coming and asking me questions not just to get answers but to set me free. I ask that when you speak to me, I would listen knowing that in your words are keys to freedom. Give me grace to not just look at my circumstances and be victimized by them but be strengthened to turn around and answer you with faith. I'm going to believe that today is the day of freedom for me.

I pray this is Jesus' Mighty Name! Amen.

In 1982, Mark Inglis and Phil Doole were high up the slopes of New Zealand's highest mountain, Aoraki Mt. Cook, when a blizzard hit.

They built an ice cave and waited for the storm to pass, but it would be 13 days before help could reach them. They survived on meager rations, but in the cramped cave, they lost circulation in their legs, which had to be amputated.

This hasn't stopped the men's climbing careers. Both have gone on to summit Mt. Cook, and in 2006, Inglis became the first double amputee to conquer Mt. Everest, losing five fingertips and more flesh off his legs to frostbite, though none of his strength of character.

He told the New Zealand Herald, "When you lose your legs when you're 23... something like this is just a minor hiccup, just a bump in the journey, really."3

Bad things happen all the time. Hard things hit us without warning. There's no way around the sin of Adam and Eve and the natural disasters of Earth. We have the liberty to believe everything "bad" always happens to us, or that

3 http://matadornetwork.com/bnt/eight-incredible-survival-stories/

"life" happens to everyone. How we choose to approach this reality will be one of the defining moments in our lives.

The definition of SURVIVOR is this: *a person who continues to function or prosper in spite of opposition, hardship, or setbacks.*

Don't you just love this? Before we break it down, let's look to the Word for more insight. Turn in your Bibles to Matthew 8 and read verses 5-13. We are going to look at a man who had a problem that he couldn't solve.

What was the main problem for this man?

_____

_____.

What do we learn he is used to seeing when he commands something?

_____

_____

_____.

What we learn is the Centurion is used to knowing what he is responsible for and doing just that to make it happen. He is used to his voice moving men. He's used to taking responsibility. He's used to doing his part so others can do theirs.

So, how does this help? How does this help him get the miracle he is in need of?

"I can't do everything but I can do something"

He couldn't solve the problem but he did what he could. He couldn't heal the servant but he went to someone who could. He didn't sit there crying, "Poor me. Why has this happened to me? What am I going to do now? Life is so hard." He may have had those thoughts initially, but eventually he went out to do something about it. He had a SURVIVOR MENTALITY: "I can't do everything but I can do something." In fact, he was so confident that if he played his role well and Jesus did His, everything could eventually work out.

Write down what he said to Jesus in verse 8.

_____

_____

_____.

Let's look at the meaning of SURVIVOR again...

SURVIVOR is a person who continues to function or prosper in spite of opposition, hardship, or setbacks. God wants you to function in your HARD THNGS. But not only that, He wants you to prosper in spite of opposition, hardship, and setback. Let's do an exercise to help us walk this out!

Make a list of the top 5 HARD THINGS you are facing right now:

1.

2.

3.

4.

5.

Take a moment and just slowly read over them. Feel the emotion that comes when you actually face the hard things in your life. It's not easy, but it's important for moving forward. It may seem simple to look at, but you're the one that has to do them and face them on a daily basis. It can be overwhelming for sure. Now, let's look at the thing we *can* do...we can start SOME-WHERE!!!

Please stop and say this out loud. (3 times)

"I don't have to do it all ... but I need to do something!"

Take the list of the 5 HARD THINGS you are facing right now from pg. 13 and write them down. Take some time to add in what you "can do" and what you "can not do."

HARD THINGS	I CAN'T DO	I CAN DO
• Centurion servant was paralyzed and in terrible suffering. He was powerless.	• Centurion could not heal his servant.	• Centurion could go to Jesus, who had the power to heal him, and ask Him to speak the Word.
• Man at Bethesda was lame for 38 years.	• Man at Bethesda couldn't heal himself.	• He could listen to exactly what Jesus asked him to do.
• My spouse and I are not getting along. We can't seem to get a breakthrough in our marriage.	• I can't change him. No matter what I say, he continues to act the same way.	• I can focus on how I act and respond to him. I'm not powerful enough to change him but I can change me.
• I had an unexpected bill come in that I can't pay. It just adds to the financial strain I'm already facing.	• I can't ignore the fact that I need to pay this bill. I can't use money I don't have.	• Be honest with myself. I need to go back and look at where I've spent my money. I need insight on what I can do without, in order to pay for what I need.
• I don't have a relationship with my Dad. He's never been a player in my life and I'm hurt by his disregard for me.	• I can't change him. I can't get him to acknowledge the fact that he has been absent from being the father I really needed.	• I can look for relationships that help fill the void I have in my heart. I can be kind to someone in the same place as I am.

MY HARD THINGS	I CAN DO	I CAN'T DO
•	•	•
•	•	•
•	•	•
•	•	•
•	•	•

CONFESS IT

I confess I'm not a victim but a survivor! I function in setbacks, opposition, hardships and thrive in difficult seasons. I am not alone. I am not called to live just surviving. I'm called to be a victor! I confess I can do all things through Christ who strengthens me and He is strengthening me right now through the inner working of His Holy Spirit. I'm looking at the list of the things I "can do" and throwing away the things "I can't." I'm called to do the very thing He's put in front of me and I'm doing it with all my might!

I declare this in Jesus' name!

PRAY IT

Lord, I'm asking you to help me do the very things in front of me. I'm understanding I'm not capable of doing all things but I can do some things and those things are right in front of me. I'm taking responsibility for the things that I can do today. I ask You to come and empower me through the grace of Your Holy Spirit to be the man/woman I'm called to be. I ask You to come into my spirit today and remind me of the things that I need to do so I can walk them out into completion.

I pray this in Jesus' name!

DAY FOUR – *GET OFF THE COUCH*

Many years ago, my sister and I decided to throw a Christmas party. Not just any party...but a glamorous dinner party! We had, admittedly, been addicted to the Food Network for some time and believed it was our turn to give it a try and wow the masses...*ok, not the masses, but twelve of our closest friends.* We went into a crazed planning mode, clipping magazine pictures, planning our four-course meal and tablescapes. It was so fun! We planned everything to the exact detail. Invitations where purchased at a high-end stationary store and sent by mail to our various friends. We tirelessly made the Chicken Cordon Bleu and fresh puff pastries for dessert.

When the day came, we were up early setting tables, cooking food, and anticipating the arrival of our guests. When the time came, a few of our friends arrived but no one else seemed to be coming. We waited and waited trying to keep the food warm and a smile on our faces until we no longer could. An hour later, with the meal partially eaten, the rest of our friends arrived. We were devastated. I don't remember all the details of what was said but the party was cut short as we ate in an awkward silence. After our guests had left, we were deflated. We sat on the couch talking about all the things that went wrong, the disappointment, and the hurt. We never threw a party like that again.

Many of us have experienced things like this in our lives. We plan for great success, preparing our lives with every detail. Not just hoping for the best, but believing we will get it. Then something happens. It's usually something that is completely out of our control. We are left hurt, disappointed, and sometimes downright devastated.

We sit on the couch of life and talk about real pain and real hurt over the circumstances we have had to walk through. It is perfectly normal and absolutely understandable to need to process and assess the wreckage. But the problem comes when we don't get up from the couch. We learn to live there. We get comfortable talking about the wrongs done to us, giving detail to every experience over and over, and nursing our pain. Then, we plan another party...yep...it's called a PITY PARTY. Yes, the one where you're the guest of honor. All things must be directed to and about you. Sadly, time flies when you're sitting on the couch of self pity. We get absorbed. We miss out. We stop living for the future and just rehearse the past.

The problem comes when we don't get up from the couch.

I need you to ask yourself a question. *Are you living in your past?*
Do your thoughts and daydreams find themselves rehearsing the past, living out each unhappy ending in your head? Are you giving yourself too much permission to sit on the couch of life and throw a pity party? Do most of your deep conversations end up reciting past failures and disappointments?

Moses had a similar "couch time" in the Book of Numbers. Take a moment to read **Numbers 11:11-15** in your own Bible.

I love how the Message phrases this passage...

Moses said to God, "Why are you treating me this way? What did I ever do to you to deserve this? Did I conceive them? Was I their mother? So why dump the responsibility of this people on me? Why tell me to carry them around like a nursing mother, carry them all the way to the land you promised to their ancestors? Where am I supposed to get meat for all these people who are whining to me, 'Give us meat; we want meat.' I can't do this by myself—it's too much, all these people. If this is how you intend to treat me, do me a favor and kill me. I've seen enough; I've had enough. Let me out of here.

One of the greatest traps of doing HARD THINGS is the "Why Me?" trap. It's a place where the enemy wants us to believe God somehow actually gave us more than we could handle and instead of being a Father to us, we are left to depend on ourselves. The enemy likes to remind us that God is not a good Father but rather a forgetful Father. Someone who likes to give us more than we can handle, only to watch and judge us for our lack of ability to follow through and do them well. It's a lie that we can easily buy into! The enemy likes us to stay in our pit. He will try to get us to buy into any lie he can to keep us bound, never victorious, and always feeling defeated. When we begin to expose the lie, we understand that the Bible says it rains on the just and the unjust. We are not being punished but simply living in a fallen world.

Once we understand this truth, it empowers us to no longer nurture our fallen souls with the "why me" but empower our spirits with the "why not" to climb out of the pit and go forward.

The enemy knows that if he can get us to take it as a personal assault from God, we will no longer believe that He is a good God but a lying and deceitful God, who likes to punish His people. If we believe this lie, we will stay in the pit and our inner lives become dark and cold without hope. We have to identify the lie of the "why me?" and understand it is a trap that will try to keep us bound. Once we understand this truth, it empowers us to no longer nurture our fallen souls with the "why me?" but empower our spirits with the "why not" to climb out of the pit and go forward.

Part of what seduces us with "why me?" is we expect a reward for our suffering. Much like our parents or friends, we expect them to turn around and feel sorry for us and somehow ease the pain and make it all better. But God is not trying to spoil you, He's trying to raise you. He's looking at you in the face and saying, "Come on! You can do this! You're the only one that can climb out of this pit. If I meet you where you are, you'll stay there!" In fact, it's His kindness that is trying to get you out of your pit. If you feel like He is not near you, I would suggest it's because He wants you to come after Him and the only way to get you out of the pit is to remove His tangible presence to cause you to run after Him and climb out of the pit.

Ok, it's time to ask yourself a few questions...

First, are you sitting on the couch of "why me" and asking everyone to come to the party, but really it's time to shut the party down and start asking "why not?"

Second, have you come to a place where you expect people to celebrate your suffering? Are you expecting others to come alongside you and nurture you in the pain?

Let's take a moment and let the Lord speak to us...

Please close your eyes and ask the Lord to show you if you are sitting on the "why me" couch in any area of your life.

If so, use your sanctified imagination and get yourself to stand up and walk away. Imagine yourself moving the couch out of your house and placing it on the corner with an attached sign saying, "FREE COUCH."

CONFESS IT

I understand HARD THINGS have happened but those things will not define me. They will not keep me from experiencing true peace in my everyday life. I'm getting up from my couch! It's been long enough and I'm ready for change! I confess I can do all things through Christ and it's time to stop asking the "why me?" and start asking "why not." It's time to start seeing my life as a victorious place and not a defeated one. I'm the only one who can climb out of this pit, so I'm taking responsibility and looking up! I'm going to stop looking for others to celebrate my brokenness and nurture my pain. I'm closing the door to this season and I'm moving on.

I declare this in Jesus' Name!

PRAY IT

Lord, I'm asking You for grace today. I understand my pain is real and the couch of "why me" feels very comfortable to sit on. I'm never going to be fulfilled if I stay here, so, I'm asking for strength to get up. I'm asking for You, Holy Spirit, to help me ask "why not" and empower me to climb out and see my life as You do. Jesus, do what You have to do! Help me climb out and see the new horizons waiting for me.

I pray this in Jesus' name!

DAY FIVE – *FULL ATTENTION*

Part of DOING HARD THINGS is understanding that in order to do HARD THINGS well, and not just have HARD THINGS happen to us, it will require our full attention.

It's normal to feel like you are a victim to hard things. It's normal to feel like all you do is survive through the hard stuff. But in order to change our mentalities, we have to give ourselves fully to the reality that Jesus wants us to live in a different place. We need a conviction that says, "I was not made to live like this."

Our job is simply to respond to this deep cry of the Spirit.

There will always be a part of us, that God-part that says we were made for more than this. It will cry out from the dark places and remind us that Jesus died to give us more. More than just surviving, more than just living. A place of deep thriving. A place of fulfillment. Our job is simply to respond to this deep cry of the Spirit. All we need to do is the very thing He's asking us to do and not anything more, with 100% commitment to full obedience. Not always seeing the end but seeing and doing the very next step. Responding with a full heart that says, "Yes!" to whatever we're asked to do.

Changing our mentality of surviving, victimization, and "Why Me" will require all that we've got! It's going to take every ounce of attention, focus, and diligence to get you out of this pit. The walls are slippery, the environment is cold, and it's dark. It's not easy to see the way out. Many times it will be the voice of the Lord simply saying the next step. Then we have to respond. There has to be an urgency in our spirit that says, "I need to make my move or I'll never get out."

Understand, many people of God spend decades in dark places, pits of pain. If we don't respond to the invitation to get out, we will die in this place. We have to see it as our only way out, our moment to respond. Our freedom is waiting!

(Turn and read Psalm 23 aloud.) Let's take a look at verse 4 in the Amplified version.

"Yes, though I walk through the [deep, sunless] valley of the shadow of death, I will fear or dread no evil, for You are with me; Your rod [to protect] and Your staff [to guide], they comfort me."

At this point, you may feel like it's deep and sunless. It may even feel like you're in a valley of death. At this point, it may seem like you don't know where to go. That is totally normal! This is why your dependency upon the

> *"You need to feel the gentle nudging of His rod, to feel the gentle push of His staff to lead you through these dark places of the unknown."*

Lord in these moments will be vital to your process of getting out. You need to feel the gentle nudging of His rod, you need to feel the gentle push of His staff to lead you through these dark places of the unknown.

This will require your full attention because you are not used to going this way. It will feel odd, uncomfortable, and at times just plain weird. But if you're committed to the process and committed to taking each step, He will lead you out. This will take you not doing "what seems right" but doing and following Who is right.

"For this very reason, adding your diligence [to the divine promises], employ every effort in exercising your faith to develop virtue (excellence, resolution, Christian energy), and in [exercising] virtue [develop] knowledge (intelligence), ..." 2 Peter 1:5 Amplified

I love how Peter puts it! We are to add diligence to our divine promises and take on every effort to exercise our faith. It will help us increase in our resolution to be free! It will cause our energy and virtue to grow. I love this point!

Diligence is a God idea! Hard work is something that He has divinely orchestrated to help us get where we need to go. So in order to get out of this pit, it's going to require you to have a diligence like you've never had before. **You were not trained for this, but you were made for this.** If you give it your full attention, you are promised freedom.

CONFESS IT

I confess I'm not afraid of hard work! I understand that God uses my diligence to equip my freedom. I respond to God's invitation to live free. I understand it will require all of my attention and focus; I am not afraid to do what He has asked. I declare I am not weak! I was made for the struggle and I can do it through Him. All my labor will lead to profit if I'm faithful in the things He's asked me to do. I declare this is the beginning of freedom and I receive grace to do His will. I declare this in Jesus' name!

PRAY IT

Lord I pray that you would release the gift of perseverance to me today. Would you fill me from within by Your spirit with supernatural perseverance and commitment to Your process and the journey of walking through hard things. Would you empower me to believe that you are leading me like a good Shepard and that You desire the best for me. Help me to choose to embrace the struggles & challenges, looking straight into Your face through it all. In Jesus name, Amen!

WEEK TWO I DO ALL THINGS

DAY SIX – *SUCCESS VS FAILURE*

Welcome to week two! I hope you had time to consider all of the mentalities that may be keeping you in the pit of pain and give yourself a chance to move forward. I know it's hard at times to identify all patterns, simple mentalities, and lifestyles, but with our determination, diligence, and the Holy Spirit's grace and perseverance, we will get out. We will be free!

Part of successfully climbing out of our pit is understanding that there is so much more waiting for us on the other side! There are many more mountains to climb, and deeper personal encounters in order to meet the love of God that waits to envelop us as we walk into eternity. It's going to be worth it!

> *"God gets more glory out of me being a success than me being a failure."*

So, we must be fully persuaded God wants our success. Our fruitfulness will bring glory to Him and His son. One of my favorite quotes is, "God gets more glory out of me being a success than me being a failure." Once we understand God uses our success to show the world His strength and glory, it allows us to enjoy seasons of struggle and believe for moments of triumph.

In John 5:20, Jesus promises us this very thing, *"For the Father loves the Son, and shows Him all things that He Himself does; and He will show Him greater works than these, that you may marvel."*

As you can see, the story of our success was in Christ's heart long ago. He saw the Father doing greater things through us than He ever did on Earth. He saw us succeeding and bringing glory to the Father even before we were born. Success means accomplishing something we set out to do. So, if the success we want is to do the very thing we were created to do and bring the Father glory, then, God wants us to be successful.

Many times our success story will begin with us doing whatever and going wherever He asks us to. We have to be committed to the process to such an extent we almost ignore the parts that seem too difficult and lean into His strength, believing He's going to use these struggles to bring glory and success to our lives.

I remember a time in my life, not too long ago, when I was really struggling with my own personal success; I was not fully convinced God wanted me to be as successful as I hoped to be. I felt a sense of loss when I would try to do

---

"You need to take yourself seriously because God does."

---

something. I would wait to see if it would happen, only to see it take so much longer than expected. I was uncertain and unsure. The Lord spoke a word into my heart that very day that marked my life. He said, *"Havilah, you need to start taking yourself more seriously, because I take you very seriously."* When He spoke those words into my spirit, I felt a gentle, yet firm, nudge of the Holy Spirit to get out there and act like the woman I was called to be. To stop waiting to be acknowledged by someone else, and accept that I was already acknowledged by the One who mattered most.

From that moment on, it didn't matter what I was doing. Whether I was writing a post, reading a book, or personally sharing my heart with someone, I began to take myself seriously. I understood God was putting a word in my heart that was meant to touch and change the world around me. I found the more I took myself seriously it allowed others to do the same. The personal confidence God had given me was now being reflected in them.

Secondly, part of our success is understanding God is waiting to be glorified. He is willing to use us to glorify Himself by using even our fragility and humanity to display His glory. If we hang out, waiting for opportunities and invitations to display His glory, we will realize that even God has to wait for divine invitations and opportunities. In the natural, it seems crazy for the God of the universe to wait for us to respond to His leadings. Perhaps most humbling is the realization that His plan is centered around using our hearts and actions to display His image and glory on Earth.

Turn in your Bible to Matthew 28:16-20

(Please take a moment and write this verse on a card)

43

As you read this passage, I want you to take a moment to make this your confession of the day. Place your hand on your heart and say this aloud...

"All authority in Heaven and on Earth has been given to me. Therefore, go and make disciples of all nations, baptizing them in the name of the Father and of the Son and of the Holy Spirit, and teaching them to obey everything I have commanded you. And surely I am with you always, to the very end of the age."

Now say, *"All authority in Heaven and on Earth has been given to me,"* again with great conviction! Say it until you know that these are not just words on a page but a promise that has power behind it. Let the Holy Spirit help you respond to this call.

I want you to write your name in the beginning of this passage:

"_____, it's time to start taking yourself more seriously, because I take you very seriously." - GOD

CONFESS IT

I declare that I am called to be a success! I am not made to sit in discouragement, failure, and defeat. Greater is He who is in me that he who is in the world. It's time for me to start living like it. I declare I am powerful in Jesus. I declare that I was created to be a carrier of the glory of God. Even today, God is anointing my heart to display His glory. I'm committed to one hundred percent obedience so that I can do and act in the way I was created. I declare today is a day of transformation.

I declare this in Jesus' name! Amen.

PRAY IT

Jesus, I ask You to help me understand how You see my own personal success. I want to see my success as You see it. I'm struck with the understanding I've sat in failure and discouragement for far too long. I've not allowed myself to fully embrace the truth that my success gives You glory. Jesus, anoint my heart for success. Anoint my actions to do the very thing You're asking me to do. I ask that You would help me deal with my past failures and current defeats. Father, help me display the glory of your son, Jesus. Transform my mind, renew my heart, and give me a right spirit to follow hard after you.

In Jesus' name! Amen.

I can do HARD THINGS because God responds to my faith and not just my failures. You are more than your last failure! You are far more than the last time you didn't believe, the last time you did what you shouldn't have, or the time you didn't step out. God sees you as a whole person. He sees your life from the end and He is trying to shepherd you from where you are now to the end of your story. He's not afraid of your failure, or that your last failure will affect His ultimate plan.

He is big enough to make anything and everything turn out for His and your good. I love the quote that says, *"He knew what He was getting when He got you. God has never been disillusioned with you, because He's never had any illusions about you."* Take a deep breath and embrace the fact that failure is part of your story.

How we handle our failures in this life are the biggest "make or break" moments we will ever have. We will all experience failure; whether we're a 'big shot' or a 'little shot,' it's coming our way! In that very moment, we can take ground or lose ground. It's as simple as that.

Two types of failures come into play. It's important to identify both.

Unforeseen Failure

The first area we experience failure is Unforeseen Failure. It's failure that happens when we least expect it. It knocks the wind out of us and knocks us off our feet. It is always very painful! We didn't expect the marriage to fail, the business to fold, the best friend to walk away, the loved one to die. Pain seems even more excruciating when we see the failure right before our eyes and yet we can do very little or nothing to change it. Overwhelmed with grief, this type of failure often begins with the phrase, *"I never saw it coming!"*

This is a moment where we need to be nice to that little girl or boy inside of us. We didn't know that we would be here. We didn't know what we would need at this very moment. It's not a time to beat ourselves up; to shame ourselves into changing. It's a moment to redefine our failures! To look that very thing in the eye that took our breath away and say, "You will not keep me down forever. I may fail but I'm not a failure. You will not define me! I will sail again." At this very moment, you can choose to exercise a new kind of faith. Faith that's more powerful than your failure. Faith that's stronger than your wounds. Faith that looks life in the eye and says, ***"My God is working it out, even if I can't see it or don't feel it. God is redefining my failure and turning it into faith!"***

48

Premeditated Failure

The second kind of failure is even harder to overcome because within it lies true motivation. The second type of failure is called Premeditated Failure. It's the kind of failure that will discount us from ever feeling like we can look at God in the face and expect anything more from Him than just surviving.

Open up your Bibles to Genesis 3:6 and read the scripture.

In this passage, we find Eve premeditating her own failure. She looked at the fruit, she thought about it, and she partook of it...even giving some to her husband. She gave into the whole thing! Eve premeditated each move as she walked right through the door of sin itself.

"You can always pick your sin, but you never get to pick your consequence."

And who could forget the most predominant, premeditated failure in the entire Bible, King David. A man sitting on the roof, watching another man's wife bathe as he lusted after her, longing to have her in his arms. Sadly, he was so powerful, he could make that desire happen. He called for her to come and he slept with her.

He even tried to cover up his own sin by having her husband murdered on a battlefield. Talk about premeditated sin! Think about the devastation of a man who wanted something so badly he was willing to put his entire morality at stake, to watch his reputation crumble right in front of him. Did King David know better? Did he understand what was at stake? Absolutely!!! David was totally aware of what he was about to do and did it anyway. I love how someone put it, *"You can always pick your sin, but you never get to pick your consequence."*

Even if we have lives filled with consequences of premeditated sin, God is still big enough to help us overcome these obstacles. If we continue to define ourselves by our personal consequences, we will never be able to walk in confidence God sees our lives as more than a payout of wrongful actions.

Let's do some work now! I want you to ask yourself a few questions:

1. *Are there failures in my life that have defined me?*

2. *Are there things that happened that I did not expect and in turn took the wind out of my sail and left me sitting on the shore?*

3. *Are there areas of premeditated failure that have left me completely devastated? Not being able to rectify the reality that Jesus came for premeditated sin as well?*

4. *Am I left living in the consequences of my premeditated sin and feel so ashamed that I don't expect anything from God other than what I have been given?*

Are you living in your past? If so, I would suggest it's hard for you to see the full work of the cross, His goodness, and His ultimate intention toward you. Your own failure has defined you. Leaving you living half a life; settling for second best.

Make a decision today to allow the Lord to help you understand you are more than your last failure. You are powerful in Jesus and full of God! The enemy has nothing on you. The cross has done its work and you are free. Even if you have consequences you are now living with, it's not the end of your story.

Lastly, we need to talk about the FAITH FACTOR. The Bible says in Hebrews chapter 11 that faith is the ultimate difference maker! When we choose to believe and operate in faith, it gets God's attention and allows Him to work and move on our behalf. Faith doesn't allow us to ignore the past or our past failures, it allows us to look far beyond them. It's like having binoculars! Faith allows us to look past the present and see into the future to all God actually has planned and will do with our failures. When we choose to operate in faith and not failure, we win, because God wins! We begin to understand our true destiny and all He has intended for us. I do not promise this will be easy, but I do know that if you use faith to see what only God can see, you will be able to overcome the great obstacles of failure. Whether they're unforeseen or premeditated, you will get through it. Faith makes the difference!

CONFESS IT

I declare I am more than my past failure! God sees me as more than my own defeat. God is working it out! I am building my faith to see past my failure and into my future. I declare the Holy Spirit is helping me to move on, to walk forward, and to live in the present with the future insight.

I declare this in Jesus name! Amen.

PRAY IT

Lord, I ask you for grace today. I understand when we talk about the failure, I have a bunch of emotions that many times rise up. I think about all the times I allowed failure to dictate my life, discourage me, overwhelm me, and lead me right into depression. I ask You to give me grace to see what I do not see. Help me believe that Your spirit is helping to work things out for my good, even in my brokenness. I also understand that with my Unforeseen Failure, it's easy to blame myself. I've expected myself to see things I could not do. Right now, I ask You to help me release myself from the burden of unexpected failure. Lord, I ask You to forgive me for picking up a burden that did not belong to me. I'm giving You back my failure and I'm accepting the work of the cross. I'm letting go and I'm leaning in to Your grace and forgiveness.

Lord, I also want to give You my Premeditated Failure. I ask for grace to walk in repentance for the things that I knew I should not have done and yet did them anyway. I know Your Word says, "If a man knows what he ought to do and does it, he sins."[4] I confess I have allowed sin in my life. I confess I have resisted the consequences of my sin. Today, I ask You to anoint my heart to receive Your forgiveness and to begin to walk in a new faith. Faith to see my future. To look past my own failures, past my own premeditated sin, and into the purposes You've created for me. I pray this in Jesus' name! Amen.

---

[4] James 4:17

DAY EIGHT – *GOD VS DEVIL*

In order to DO HARD THINGS well we must recognize there is a real enemy to our destiny. He is a liar and a thief (see John 10:10). He would love nothing better than to define you by your failures. Reminding you that your "label" is Failure, and that your true nature, at the end of the day, is to fail and you can't change. Remember he is a LIAR! He doesn't have to speak the truth, he just needs you to believe his lies.

> *"He doesn't have to speak truth he just needs to get you to believe his lies."*

The first thing the devil wants to do in your life is render you powerless. He wants you to buy into the lie that you are still fighting for your victory and if you work hard enough or try hard enough, you may succeed. It is a lie. **You are not working "for" victory, you are working "from" victory. You're not working "for" love, you are living as someone who "is" loved.** He wants you to be exasperated trying everything and anything to make you win. You have already won! The Bible teaches that the devil is under your feet and you do not need to fight for victory anymore. You *are* victorious! This doesn't mean we don't have to renew our minds or transform the way we act *(we'll talk about this in a bit)* but ultimately, we have a new heart with the Spirit of God working within us. So, freedom is already our portion. Victory is already at hand.

Romans 8:11 says, *"The same power that raised Christ from the dead is now living within us."* That same power that took Jesus out of the grave is now enabling us to walk out of our own graves. Death could not hold Him and neither can it hold us. This power is at our disposal 24 hours a day, 7 days a week, 365 days a year...at any moment you need it. It is a force to be reckoned with and it is yours. Nothing can ever harm your soul again!

1 John 5:4 reminds us, *"Everyone born of God overcomes the world."* The devil believes that the Earth is his and everything in it. He thinks, *"just because you are in the world you are of the world."* He is wrong. You now belong to Jesus. Jesus paid the price for your soul. When Jesus died on the cross and took your punishment for the sins you committed (unforeseen and premeditated), you were instantaneously set free. All of Earth's customs and superficial ways of living are no longer what matters to us. What Jesus died to give us is the biggest reality in our lives!

In the previous chapter, John also reminds us, "Greater is He who is in us than he who is in the world." The enemy will want you to believe the darkness and evil in this world have the same power as God and His Heavenly host. The truth is, the devil is not a god. He is a fallen angel. God is the only one true God. He stands alone. The devil's destiny is set and he goes straight to Hell when Jesus returns.

One of the primary weapons the enemy has is FEAR. He loves to paralyze the people of God with fear. Causing us to stop fighting from a place of victory and getting down in the trenches with him and his demons. Listen! It's your time to climb up on the mountain of faith. Take a look at the world from how God sees it. He loves the world and He's giving every person in the world every chance to choose Him before He returns. But God isn't worried if the devil is going to win and if we will lose. Nevertheless, our complete victory will require serious diligence and a commitment to not be dominated by the seductions in this world.

The Bible gives us the perfect analogy for us to hold on to. It says we are in the world but we are no longer of it. I love the way The Message says it:

"Friends, this world is not your home, so don't make yourselves cozy in it. Don't indulge your ego at the expense of your soul. Live an exemplary life among the natives so that your actions will refute their prejudices. Then they'll be won over to God's side and be there to join in the celebration when he arrives." 1 Peter 2:11

This picture describes someone who is visiting a land but not staying there. We were created to bless and serve those who are native to this planet, but dreaming and preparing for another place...reminding those we serve they are welcome to come as well.

How you choose to live is the biggest decision you get to make. You can live powerless or powerful, fearful, or faith-filled. You can determine to climb the mountain or you can hang out in the valley with your friends, coworkers, parents and never see the life you were intended to live. God did not send His only son to die an excruciating death so you can live fighting a devil, believing his lies, and keeping you down. The greatest way you can celebrate Jesus and the cross is to acknowledge what He did and to live a life worthy of the calling you received. (see Ephesians 4:1)

Speak to God right now aloud and say this.

CONFESS IT

I confess today that Jesus is my King! The devil doesn't own me and he never will. Just because I'm on the Earth doesn't make me his, and he has no right to dictate how I'm going to live. God is big enough, great enough, and strong enough to keep me safe, sound, and secure, all the days of my life. Jesus, I believe in you. I trust you. And I'm leaning on You to do the right thing until You come. I declare this in Jesus' name! Amen.

PRAY IT

Jesus, I ask You to help me to believe You in a greater way. I understand the devil wants me to believe his lies and live defeated and discouraged. I am not going to buy into them any longer. I ask You to help me see the devil as he really is, a liar. Help me to identify his lies that keep me defeated. I want to believe the truth, to walk in those things You have made for me. Help me to believe who You created me to be, and not defend lies that assault me.

Lord, I ask You for a greater grace to walk in truth. I ask You for a greater capacity to identify lies that keep me bound. Give me a supernatural understanding to look and see what these seducing lies look like and to reject them. I asked this in Your mighty name! Amen.

DAY NINE – WEAPON OF FEAR

Yesterday, we talked about God being stronger than the devil. It's important to understand just because we win, doesn't mean we can't feel or experience defeat in the process. The devil has weapons and they are fashioned to hurt us. Bishop T. D. Jakes says it well, "You must understand your enemy, for you cannot defeat what you do not understand."

"The enemy has weapons which he uses to keep us from believing we are powerful."

We can DO HARD THINGS when we believe no weapon formed against us will prosper. But in order for them not to prosper we have to understand how they operate. The Bible challenges us to not be ignorant of the devil's schemes or devices. The enemy has weapons which he uses to keep us from believing we are powerful...deceived into underestimating our own spiritual strength.

You see, if we believe we are weak, even if we possess strength, we will still act weak. The devil knows if he can deceive us in our weakness, in our brokenness, and in our guilt, we will never be effective for the Kingdom of God. The devil doesn't have many weapons, but the ones he does have he uses often. The Bible says that the serpent was the most crafty of all animals. He had an ability to dupe Adam and Eve out of the promises of God. Let's be honest, if he can do it to Adam and Eve, he could definitely do it to us.

Today, I want us to look at the weapon of fear. It's a stronghold that likes to come and wrap its arms around our heart, mind, and strength, to keep us bound from operating in the strength we possess. Fear says 'we are not going to make it', 'things are not going to work out,' 'we are never going to live a good life', and 'if the worst happens, you will not be able to survive.' These are lies that come straight out of the devil's mouth to keep us from being all we're called to be. 1 John 4:18 tells us tormenting fear never comes from God.

> *"Faith increases by listening and believing as does fear."*

One thing that helped me early on was understanding that fear increases in the same way faith does. Faith increases by listening and believing, as does fear. If all you're listening to is fear-based, eventually, you will begin to believe it. Once you understand this, you can start to value what you're listening to and letting into your life. You see, many times, we are inundated with information sounding truthful and we begin to believe it. If the market's falling apart, our lives are falling apart. If they can't heal your sickness, you can never be healed. If your kid is ADHD, he's never going to be able to concentrate because the professionals said so. As we discussed yesterday, we are no longer bound by what the world says. We are bound by what God says! Our reality is now shaped by our theology. And if He said it, it's as good as done.

We need to increase our faith and not just reject fear. The best weapon against fear is increased faith. Don't just tell yourself to stop fearing, tell your inner man to start believing! Read, listen to, and say faith-filled statements.

Practice speaking like a spirit-filled person. If you would normally say something that is fearful or worrisome, stop yourself. Remember, we believe what we hear...even from our own mouths. Yes, it's going to take practice. It's a spiritual exercise and it doesn't come overnight. But I promise you, and, more importantly, the Bible promises you, that Faith comes by hearing the Word of God. Fill your mouth with the Word and your faith will grow. Guaranteed!

Fear means to shrink back and run. That's why the Bible says, "Fear not!" It means don't run, shrink back, or give up. It's important to understand when fear comes, our first objective many times is to run. We want to get as far away from the pain of the unknown as we can.

How do we stop from running when fear hits us? I like to think of it this way: we have to have a plan to deal with fear! Remember, when fear comes, initially we feel paralyzed, dumbfounded, and overwhelmed. It's important for us to plan for these emotions and understand it is just anxiety. These emotions cannot dominate us. The first thing we need to tell ourselves is, "This is anxiety. I have done nothing wrong, and I am not in trouble. I can do this!" Once we talk ourselves down, we need a plan to get out of fear. It may be planning to read a certain passage in the Bible, listen to a certain worship song, or pray out loud and declare truth over ourselves.

We have to go after fear and not allow it to immobilize us. Don't be surprised if it feels awkward at first. Remember, we are learning to operate in our spiritual authority and with our spiritual weapons; it won't come naturally at first, but like that classic quote says, "Practice makes perfect," and it is true with this.

Transformation is as practical as it is spiritual.

Transformation is as practical as it is spiritual. Sometimes, we have to practically set up objectives for our success and that is spiritual. Don't let the enemy lie to you that you need to have some sort of spiritual high to get you out of the pit. All you need to do is listen to the Holy Spirit, obey exactly what He's asking you to do, and set God boundaries to keep yourself safe. You can do this! I promise.

So let's do some work, let me ask you these simple questions:

1. Are you allowing the weapon of fear to dominate your life?

2. Do you find yourself being dominated by anxiety about your future?

3. Do you have a plan to get yourself away from the weapon of fear?

It's okay if you don't, but do start today.

I want you to take a moment and simply write down a plan for the next time you sense fear coming your way.

When fear comes, the best thing for me to do is…

_____

_____

_____

_____

_____

_____.

When fear comes, the worst thing for me to do is…

_____

_____

_____

_____

_____

_____

_____.

When fear comes, I will not allow myself to…

_____

_____

_____

_____

_____

_____

When fear comes, I will allow myself to…

_____

_____

_____

_____

_____

_____

_____.

C O N F E S S   I T

I confess perfect love casts out all fear! Today, I am leaning into the love of the Father and kicking out fear in Jesus' name. I understand that the devil has very few weapons to use and one of them is fear. I will not allow it. Fear has no place in my heart, mind, or strength. I was made to be brave! I was made to walk in courage. What God says shapes the way I see my life. Today, I'm increasing my faith by listening, singing, and declaring the Word of God. I've got a plan to get me out of fear and I'm going to use it. Devil, you better watch out, because I will no longer be manipulated by you.

I declare this in Jesus' name! Amen.

PRAY IT

Lord, I ask You to help me today! I recognize fear has come to torment me, control me, and manipulate me. I ask You to help me see what I cannot and believe there is a way out. I'm beginning to understand when I allow fear in, it kicks You out. I ask You to forgive me. I ask You to remind me, even today, how to use my plan to get out of fear. Please show me specific ways to believe You more and to grow my faith. I also understand I can be so dominated by fear that I make decisions out of it. I ask You to make a way where there is no way and show me how to obey You more. Give me grace to do Your will.

I pray this in Jesus' name! Amen.

DOING HARD THINGS will be one of the hardest things you will ever face, but doing them while struggling with unbelief will make it nearly impossible. Without a believing heart, it's impossible to understand why our struggles happen in the first place, why God would allow them, and how they will work for our good. One of the strongest weapons the enemy uses against us is unbelief. Unbelief is deadly to a Christian and deadly to your heart.

In fact, in the book of Revelations, verse 21:8, it says that eternal security is not given to the unbelieving. Wow! It's that serious. It means that if we do not recognize and deal with unbelief and doubt, we may suffer eternal consequences. So today, we are going to take a look at this weapon called "unbelief" and begin to deal with it swiftly. I believe doubt and unbelief have to be dealt with quickly before they take root and grow into a weed that chokes out God's life in us. (See Matthew)

The word *doubt* means *to waiver and hesitate, to fluctuate in opinion*. One of the dangers of doubt is that we believe what's being said or seen over the Word of God. Doubt gives us reason to waiver, hesitate, and fluctuate with common opinion or conventional wisdom. It's a dangerous place to be. It means whomever you hang out with, listen to, or whatever you allow to dominate your life changes your belief system and values. Eventually, it changes your attitudes and personality to believe or disbelieve the truth.

Doubt is a sin that leads us away from God. It causes us to walk away from believing what He is saying because we can't see it. Remember, as Hebrews Chapter 11 so clearly teaches: faith is the evidence of things not yet seen, and yet still believing. This is the danger of doubt. Doubt tells us that if we can't see it, touch it, taste it, or feel it, then it's not real. It is deadly and we must recognize and deal with it quickly.

> *"Lazy people often struggle with unbelief because they don't want to take the time to develop faith."*

Lazy people often struggle with unbelief because they don't want to take the time to develop faith. Yes, I said it! Lazy people. Apathetic people who are not willing to take the time to search what the Word says, to ask the questions and to patiently wait for the answers. Having faith and belief is a matter of maturity. It's allowing ourselves to grow in our belief system and letting our roots go down deep so we can bear the fruit that only comes through faith, believing, hoping, and trusting in God. So, when the winds and waves of unbelief and doubt come crashing in upon us, we won't waver. We refuse to be caught up in such foolishness, but chose to stand firm believing in the impossible. Trusting in the impossible dream that the God of the possible can make it happen.

The Bible also talks about unbelief in Hebrews 4:11; it will shut out the promises of God in our lives. Let's read this together...

"For we also have had the good news proclaimed to us, just as they did; but the message they heard was of no value to them, because they did not share the faith of those who obeyed." Hebrews 4:11

I love how the Amplified version of the Bible elaborates this point. It says *they did not share the faith,* and then in parentheses it says this...*with the leaning of the entire personality on God in absolute trust and confidence in His power, wisdom, and goodness.* This perfectly depicts what faith actually is. It's a leaning on the entire personality of God in absolute trust and confidence in Him; confidence in His power, wisdom, and goodness.

"True trust is believing God's intentions towards you are always good."

A couple of years ago, I was riding my bike, talking to God about the issue of trust in my life. I remember expressing to Him that I really wanted to know what trust was and what it was to trust Him. I remember Him saying this exact phrase to me, "Havilah, true trust is believing that my intentions towards you are always good." I was struck at that moment with the meaning. I felt His words read me like a book. If I really trusted Him, I would believe in His intentions and that they were good. It placed a magnifying glass on every aspect of my life and caused me to want to change. In fact, it magnified the areas of unbelief I had been hiding in my own heart, thinking they were not a very big deal to Him. If we say we love someone and trust them, but underneath it all, we doubt their intentions are good toward us, we really don't trust them. This was all I needed to hear to empower me to get unbelief out of my heart and to begin to believe Him again.

My question to you today is: do you believe God's intentions towards you are completely good? I hope this question magnifies your own areas of doubt and unbelief.

My second question is: are you leaning on God's intentions? Do you not just *say* He is good but are you setting your life to rely upon His goodness?

"Clarity is a gift given to those who believe and have faith in God."

Another aspect of unbelief I want to talk about today is the tormenting spirit of *confusion*. It's a spirit I believe the enemy uses to keep us from reaching clarity. Clarity is a gift given to those who believe and have faith in God. Clarity gives us a clean mind; that sees things clearly and is not caught up in confusion, wavering, and doubt, leading us away from God. It can cause us to search out clarity in places other than the Bible and His Spirit's voice. This is why it is so important that we know the Word and the Word knows us. The Word of God is the only thing that can give us God Himself here on Earth.

I love the phrase, "There is a man between the pages." I believe the Word of God speaks to us, reads us, and gives us discernment in our heart, mind, and motives. It allows us to clearly see what needs to be seen. Confusion is a lying spirit; it says, "You'll never know. You are doomed to live in doubt." God is not the author of doubt. He is not the author of confusion, or even hesitation. He knows *what* He wants, *when* He wants it, and *how* He's going to do it. God has placed His spirit within us to help us receive that very thing we've been promised. You've been promised clarity! It's God's gift to you.

2 Corinthians 14:33 explicitly states that God is not the author of confusion. If God has not authored confusion, we can clearly know where it comes from: the devil! He uses confusion as a weapon to keep us from believing and receiving all we've been promised.

CONFESS IT

I declare today that I am God's! The Spirit of God is living within me and He is helping me to believe for greater things. I will not give in to doubt, fear, hesitation, or lack of clarity. I have been promised a clear mind and that is what I'm receiving. I will not be apathetic in my pursuit of Christ! I'm pressing into the greater things and building my faith in order to destroy the enemy's weapons against me.

I declare this in Jesus' name! Amen.

PRAY IT

Jesus, I come to You and I ask You for grace today. I understand the enemy uses doubt and unbelief to hurt me, to cause me to doubt who You are, and to bring me pain. I ask You to help me climb out of the pit of unbelief and doubt. I ask You to empower me to strengthen my faith. Renew a right spirit within me, so that I may seek hard after God and find Him. I confess that I have tried to make doubt a friend. I confess I've allowed unbelief to rule my heart and my mind. Today, I'm putting a stop to it. I ask You to give me an understanding and believing heart to see You and to know You in a greater way.

I pray this in faith! Amen.

WEEK THREE I DO SOME THINGS

Welcome to week three!!! I hope you have been enjoying I DO HARD THINGS. During the previous two weeks, we've explored the topics of *Doing Hard Things* and *Doing All Things*. Now, we are going to explore *Doing Some Things* this week.

If you remember, during our first week, we talked about the man in the Bible who could do some things but not everything. This is a godly concept. Your inability to do everything well, all the time, is part of your makeup. When God created you, He did not create you with boundless energy and open-ended freedom so you could run here and there, keeping yourself busy all the time. He created you with purpose and part of that purpose has to do with boundaries. I love the quote: *"God doesn't have to abuse you to use you."* He's not looking for workers; He's looking for sons and daughters. God Himself understands limits and boundaries because He created them and works within them Himself. Let's take a look at some of the boundaries God created, and the limits He operates within.

Turn in your Bibles to **Revelations 3:20** and read the passage…

This is God speaking and He says, "Behold, I stand at the door and knock." God is standing at the door of our hearts and is knocking. We see that He is pursuing and initiating here but then we see our part in the next line: "If anyone hears my voice and opens the door...." This is our part. It is our job to hear the knock and open the door. God does not force His way in. He doesn't plow down the door to get into our hearts and minds to make Him Lord. He simply knocks and waits. This is called a boundary.

We see in the next phrase, He says, "I will come in and dine with him." We see again that open invitation, God walks through the door and sits and eats with us. God is showing us boundaries. He's expressing limits. He is saying this is where you begin and I end, or, this is where I begin and you end. It is a dance of boundaries, limits, invitations, yeses and no's. God has no interest in violating our boundaries.

Let's read about a rich young ruler to whom Jesus gave this invitation. Turn in your Bibles to **Matthew 10:17-27** and read the story.

We see Jesus tells the young ruler the hard truth and sets a firm boundary. He says, "Sell all you have and give to the poor, and you will have a treasure in Heaven." He makes a boundary; making it exceedingly clear that the man has to do this in order to have that. The rich young ruler then rejects the invitation, "...he went away sad, because he had great wealth."

Let me ask you a few questions:

Did Jesus initiate the conversation?

Did Jesus ask the young man to do something only he could do?

When the man walked away sad, did Jesus run after him?

Did Jesus interrupt His command to make the young man happy?

All of these answers have a resounding...**No!**

You see, many of us expect God to interrupt His commands to keep us happy. But when we read this story in the Bible, it does not offend us. We clearly see Jesus was setting a limit on what He could provide for the man. The rich young ruler had the power to make his own decision. Jesus set a boundary. He will always set limits on what He will do and what we need to do. Was the man powerless? Absolutely not! He had every right to make any decision he chose, but he likewise had to accept what Jesus said. Jesus was not going to break His limits in order to keep the man happy.

We see this throughout the entire Bible. God never invades our personal choice or will. He initiates. He knocks. He speaks the truth, and then He leaves it up to us to make a decision. Even the people of Israel were given a free will and choice that dictated their path.

Lastly, think about the story in Genesis that talks about Adam and Eve and the Tree of the Knowledge of Good and Evil in the Garden of Eden. This is a clear story of how God used boundaries and limits without control. God clearly outlined to Adam and Eve they could have anything in the whole garden except the fruit of the Knowledge of Good and Evil. Adam and Eve used their free will and freedom to eat the fruit. God did not strike them with lightning when they grabbed the fruit. He did not blind them in the midst of their decision. He simply said, "If you eat of this tree, there will be consequences."

When God finally found them hiding in the garden, He asked them questions that revealed their heart. Even though they were afraid and ashamed, He continued with His boundary. He cast them out of the garden and gave them each consequences for their sin. He was a good father. A good father follows through with what He says. So when He speaks, we trust Him. If He doesn't follow through, we wouldn't trust Him. God, even though it was excruciating, followed through with what He had said. He understood boundaries and limits, establishing a very clear "yes" and "no."

So today, you need to see God as a good Father, not a controlling master; to understand He has boundaries and limits and they are part of His commitment to keep us safe. If He allowed everything, all of the time, and never followed through with what He said, we would be in big trouble. It is His kindness and love that sets boundaries.

CONFESS IT

I confess I do need limits! I am created in the image and likeness of a good God. He would not tell me "no" unless it was for my safety. I'm determined to only do what God is asking me to do. When God says "stop," I will stop. When God says "go," I go. I will only do what I see my Father doing. I will not hold God to a double standard. I will not hold Him responsible for my happiness, without my obedience.

I declare this in Jesus' name! Amen.

PRAY IT

Lord, I thank You that You are helping me to understand that I cannot do all things, that I can only do some things. I ask that You will continue to invite me into this new life of godly boundaries, limits, and invitations. I ask that You will reveal the areas I have not had or accepted Your boundaries. I confess I have not seen Your limits as part of Your love and Your safety toward me. I ask You to help me continue to be the person You've asked me to be. Help me see You as a loving Father and when I hear a "no" to respond well. Thank You for setting up this whole system to keep me safe, and to let me know that You are God who does not lie.

I pray this in Jesus' name! Amen.

DAY TWELVE – *I Can Do Some Things*

"Others can, but I cannot." This phrase was used a lot in our home growing up. I didn't understand its truth until I was much older. It holds a huge godly principle talked about in the Bible in 1 Corinthians 10:23. Please open up your Bible and read the passage...

I love how the Amplified version states it...

"All things are legitimate [permissible—and we are free to do anything we please], but not all things are helpful (expedient, profitable, and wholesome). All things are legitimate, but not all things are constructive [to character] and edifying [to spiritual life]."

Part of having godly boundaries is understanding that we were not created to do all things, and all things are not helpful for us. There are a bunch of things that we can all do according to the Bible but they're not always helpful for us. Part of being a spiritual grownup is understanding what is not only permissible for us but what actually is helpful. What are the things that keep our lives profitable and wholesome? What actually helps us construct good character and edifies our spiritual life? It is your job as a spiritual adult to figure out what these things are. It is also each of our jobs to figure out what is not helpful to us...the things we can all do, but shouldn't.

When it comes to boundaries, only you, with the help of the Holy Spirit, will be able to set them at a healthy place. Your life, time, and relationships are yours alone and they require tailor-made boundaries and limits. My boundaries and limits will not work in your life or yours in mine. This is why it is crucial that we personally cooperate with the Holy Spirit and the Word to give us clear boundaries. Tomorrow, we will talk about what the Bible says should be within our boundaries and what are non-negotiable. But today, I want to talk about this truth: just because we can do something doesn't always mean we should.

Turn your Bible to **Galatians 6:2-5** and read it...

In this passage, it clearly outlines some boundaries, limits, and property lines we all should be operating in. Paul says in the first phrase, "Carry each other's burdens." The word *burden* here means *an excessive and crushing load*. It gives us the picture of a huge boulder. Paul is saying if you see someone who has a crushing and excessive boulder in their life, help them! Don't leave them! Helping others do what they cannot do for themselves is sacrificial love and honors God. Paul is stating that we are responsible "to" each other. We are each other's family and when someone is hurting, it is our job to help them. But only for a short time.

We'll talk more about this in a moment...

Verse 5 states, "Each one should carry their own load." The word *load* means *a burden or cargo of daily toil*. It gives us a picture of a backpack. Paul is saying each of us should carry the backpack, or the daily toil, we've been given. He states we are all expected to carry our own load. So, when we see someone who is working hard and laboring over their daily tasks, it is what God designed them to do. Labor and hard work are part of God's plan and it's important we don't step in the way of it. If carrying each other's boulder is being responsible "to" someone, then letting someone carry their own burden and/or backpack is not being responsible "for" someone.

The Bible is saying we each are to carry our own load. But if someone gets in trouble with something that is too big to take care of on their own, we can step in for a moment and help them. But we are not created to carry everyone else's backpack. They were created for theirs. We get in trouble when we begin to take everyone else's load and make it ours. God specifically designed a load for you. This backpack is part of His design and it keeps us dependent upon Him for our daily happenings.

So we have to ask ourselves these questions:

Am I carrying someone else's backpack around?

Am I allowing myself to ease someone else's load and it's keeping them a spiritual infant?

Am I allowing them to grow in strength and endurance by carrying their own load?

Secondly, is there someone around me I'm helping who has a crushing burden?

Am I expecting them to do something I myself would not be able to do without help?

Lastly, is it time to give the burden back?

Was it a crushing boulder that has now become a backpack?

Is it affecting the way I do life and my own ability to carry my own load?

Today, I want you to take some time and really evaluate and answer the questions above. God has not asked you to be a savior to the world. He is! That role has already been taken.

As you have answered the questions above, I want you to understand something. If you continue to hold someone else's backpack for very long time, you will not be able to carry your own load as well. God did not create you to carry more than you can hold. So, for some of us, it will require us being more obedient to God. It may require you understanding that you are not more productive, more valuable, and more blessed because you are doing things for others that they should be doing for themselves. In fact, you may be getting in the way of what God is trying to do in them. I know this may not have been your understanding up until this point, but now you know what God expects and it's time to change.

CONFESS IT

I declare even though I can do a lot of things, I am not called to do everything. I understand the seduction of carrying more than my load will keep me bound and disobedient to what God is asking of me. I confess I am not made to carry other people's burdens! Today, I am giving them back. I'm putting on my own backpack. It alone is manageable for me. I understand if someone has a crushing load, I can step in, but only for a short time. I must give it back in due season. I will not walk around with other people's backpacks. I will not hinder other's growth because I want to be a savior. Jesus, you are the Savior of the world and I give you back that role.

I declare this in Jesus' name! Amen.

PRAY IT

Lord, I'm asking for Your help today. I understand I can easily be seduced into carrying more than what you've asked me to. At times, I have taken other people's burdens and backpacks to help them or to ease my own anxiety. But today I want to choose to be obedient. I want to walk in the way

You've asked me to and that is to simply carry my own load. Lord, I ask that You would give me eyes to see those who have crushing boulders. Give me grace to help them for a season but when the appropriate moment comes, help me to give it back. I am committed to 100% obedience and want to be more concerned about honoring You than honoring them. Help me to be a tool in Your hand, ready to do Your will and not hindering the things placed before each of us.

I asked us in Your name! Amen.

DAY THIRTEEN – *I DO BOUNDARIES*

Proverbs 25:28 says, *"Like a city whose walls are broken down is a man who lacks self-control."* Each of us has been given boundaries. A boundary is like a property line or a city wall. These walls have been designed to keep in what is supposed to stay inside and keep out what is supposed to stay outside. I like to call it our personal yard. The term "yard" is a borrowed term but I think it perfectly depicts what we're talking about today.

God has designed a "yard" for you. Your yard has an invisible gate around it and within it lies the things God holds you personally responsible for. There are things God will hold you responsible for in your life that He will hold no one else responsible for. It doesn't matter if you've never been told these things before today; as we talk about them, you will begin to see what God sees. The things He's asking you to manage can be done well if given your full attention. As we look at our personal yards today, I want you to understand, like the Bible teaches, our yards will be broken down without self-control. It takes extreme self control to keep them safe. It takes boundaries to keep you safe. It will require obedience to keep you safe. People who lack boundaries often lack obedience. Any healthy relationship has a healthy boundary.

Your yard holds three specific areas you are responsible for:

Feelings

The first part of your yard that you are responsible for is your FEELINGS. Your feelings are yours and you have the right to feel whatever you want to feel. But you have to understand that those feelings are yours and are entirely chosen by you. Our feelings are like a dashboard. They allow us to understand what is going on inside our soul. They tell us if something needs attention. If we have a feeling that rises up that surprises us, it's a good indicator that there's something that needs our attention and we must look into it. If we do not allow ourselves to feel specific things, we are not respecting ourselves. It is not respectful to not allow a feeling. But once we have that feeling, we get to choose how we interpret it. Are we going to stay angry? Are we going to feel disrespected? Are we going to choose to feel hurt or choose empathy? There are a plethora of feelings that come to us everyday but we have the power to choose whatever feelings we want to stay.

It's also important to understand that no one can make you feel anything. No one can make you feel powerless. No one can make you feel helpless. No one can make you angry. No one is that powerful. You get to choose your feelings. They are yours and yours alone, and they are to be respected. But no one is powerful enough to go into your yard and make you feel any certain way. If you have allowed others to dictate your feelings, it's time to take your power back. I want you to say, "No one is powerful enough to make me feel any certain way. I'm getting my power back! If I want to be sad and feel mad, that is about me. I understand now and own it. No one can make me feel hurt. Yes, they can hurt me and hurt might be my initial feeling, but I can choose to feel a different way about it in the end."

Attitudes

The second area in our yard God holds us responsible for is the area of our ATTITUDES. Your attitude is in your yard; it's yours and you own it. Attitudes come from various places but primarily they come from our values and our belief systems. Whatever we believe and value eventually seeps into our attitudes and our feelings. This is why it is important that we don't just try to change our attitudes but we reevaluate our belief systems and our values because they will eventually change our attitudes.

If you have a bad attitude, it's yours and you've chosen to have it. This should concern you! If you have a good attitude, it's yours and you've chosen to have it. This should empower you! The Holy Spirit wants to help you have the attitude that helps you prosper and grow. The Word of God helps us understand what a godly attitudes are and how to keep them. Today, the attitudes you have are because you have chosen them. They are fully yours, allowing you to act any way you want to. Choose wisely!

Choices

The third and final area God holds us responsible for is our CHOICES. Whatever we choose to do and the actions we take are fully ours. Once we are adults, whatever we choose to do is our responsibility. We need to take 100% responsibility for our choices and the choices we need to make in order to change and grow. We cannot blame our actions on anyone else other than ourselves. God holds us responsible for each choice we make. God chooses the consequences of our actions but ultimately our actions are in our yard. No longer can we look at the person next to us and blame them for the decisions we've made. Our spouse is not responsible. Our parents are not responsible. We are! Your choices, whether you believe it or not, are in your yard and God holds you responsible for them now.

With that said, we have a lot to do. If you manage your boundaries well, you will have very little time for anything else. It will take almost 100% of your attention to focus on your feelings, attitudes, and choices and manage them well. This is a good thing! God would not ask you to do something you cannot do well. God's Spirit will help us manage our yards in such a way that we can maintain peace, joy, and freedom the whole time. This will require a tremendous amount of self-control and discipline on our part.

Maintaining healthy boundaries will require us to stay fully awake in our daily lives, recognizing feelings that want to take root and poison our hearts. It will require an ability to reevaluate our attitudes, going deep into our values and belief systems to root out an unbelieving or critical spirit. It will also require us to operate as spiritual adults and understand that all of our choices, whether past, present or future, are ours. We get to own them and we will reap their fruit as well.

One of the greatest struggles in the Christian life, when it comes to boundaries, is not always understanding that others will want to put their feelings, attitudes, and choices in your yard. They will have no problem expecting you to manage their feelings, to put up with their attitudes, and to have insight into their choices. It's easy for them to see you as responsible, especially if you are a very responsible person. It will require you, working with the Holy Spirit, to maintain healthy boundaries. You will have to talk to yourself. You will need to tell yourself things like, *"I cannot make anyone feel anything. I am not that powerful"* and *"I have done nothing wrong, I am not in trouble. This is anxiety."* Once you understand that other people would love you to carry their burden, you will be able to discern when the enemy is trying to burden you with things that God has not asked you to carry.

It is best at this point to not try and verbally shove everyone's attitudes, feelings, and choices back into their yard but rather privately and prayerfully ask the Holy Spirit to help you firmly and gently keep your boundaries clear. Our motive should always be one of obedience. We need to set our hearts on the reality that God created boundaries to keep us safe and our lives manageable. We were not designed to live without boundaries and if we do, it will hurt us. We need to see that having a lack of boundaries is not only disobedient but also harmful to our spiritual lives. Tomorrow, we will talk about setting limits, but today I want us to evaluate our own personal boundaries and boundary lines.

As babies, we do not get to choose our choices, attitudes, or feelings, but now that we are adults, we do. So, like the Bible says, "Choose this day whom you will serve.[5]" I believe it is that simple. Are we committed to managing our choices, feelings, and attitudes in such a way that pleases God and demonstrates a manageable, peaceful, and love-filled life? If you want to be more like God, then have more boundaries.

CONFESS IT

I declare I'm getting my yard back! I was not created to feel powerless. With the help of the Holy Spirit and good, old-fashioned effort, I'm going to manage my feelings, choices, and attitudes in a pleasing way before the Lord. I am no longer willing to blame anyone for my yard. I'm going to show up like a grown-up and govern my yard with my full attention. Enemy, you can no longer tell me the lie that my feelings, attitudes, and choices are beyond my control. God has given me every tool to take care of them well and today, by making a change, I'm committed to full obedience.

I declare this in Jesus name! Amen.

---

[5] Joshua 24:15

94

PRAY IT

Lord, I look to You today. I understand my yard can seem overwhelming without Your wisdom to know what needs to be in it, and what doesn't. I ask You for supernatural discernment to understand where my property line begins and where it ends. I ask You to empower me to do the right thing; to give others their feelings back and for me to own mine. I ask You to give me wisdom to see where my belief systems have led me to cling to attitudes that have harmed me. I want to change! I ask You to help me show up like a spiritual grown-up and own my choices for what they are. I will no longer render myself as powerless in the midst of my daily living! I accept the Holy Spirit's empowerment to live the life I'm called to live with godly boundaries, and a well managed yard.

I pray this in Jesus' name! Amen.

Part of Doing Some Things well is understanding we have to walk within boundaries. Yesterday, we talked about what God holds us personally responsible for. Today, I want to talk a little bit about personal limits. The limits we set for ourselves and others.

The benefit to having limits or boundaries is it allows the good to stay in and the bad to stay out. These boundaries are not solid walls but rather fences with gates. The gates help our boundaries breathe, allowing the things we want to stay in, without shutting everything out. It's important that our boundaries breathe. Godly boundaries do not look like massive cement walls but rather fences that open and close, allowing people and things in and out for certain times and seasons.

Setting limits are very important and a godly attribute. There are two types of limits I want to talk about today:

Limits on Others

The first is setting limits on others. Now, I say that tongue-in-cheek because it's impossible to set limits on others. Remember we are not powerful enough to control someone else's actions. However, we can set limits on our exposure to other people who are behaving poorly. We don't have to be around people who do not respect who we are and the boundaries we set. There is no Biblical law that says others can treat us poorly and that we must receive it because it makes us seem more spiritual. We can hang out with people who behave poorly but it's entirely up to us and it should be on a limited basis. The Bible says we are to separate ourselves from people who act in destructive ways. We are not being unloving, we are simply setting boundaries. In fact, we are loving ourselves well!

Separation allows us to protect and love because we are taking a stand against the things that can potentially destroy. The enemy would love you to believe a lie that you must be around people who treat you without love or even harmfully. He'll say you are not being kind if you do not allow them in. This is a lie. God does not treat or train His children with abuse. God does not teach kindness by meanness, or love by cruelty. This is not a picture of a kind Father. We need to be careful who we allow to hang out in our yards, even who we allow to speak into our yards. God does not always set limits for Himself, but He does set standards. He limits His exposure to evil, unrepentant people and so should we.

Communicating boundaries is essential in order to DO HARD THINGS. Successful people know how to do this and they do it well. They don't have to yell their boundaries or blame someone else (like a spouse) but they can simply say "no" or "not now" and mean it. It's important for us to use boundary words like "no." "No" is a boundary word and it communicates a property line. You will know if you are not operating as an adult with boundaries when the person you are setting boundaries for causes you to change your 'no' to a 'yes'. As long as you don't change your resolve, you have not lost your voice. Part of communicating boundaries is letting others know what they can and cannot do. If they are unwilling to respect your boundaries, they should not have the privilege of being around you.

I know some of you are thinking, "But what if it is my spouse? How do I get away from them! What if they don't respect my boundaries?" Let me start by saying it's going to take some time for you to reestablish your boundaries with those closest to you. Remember, it took a long time for you to get to this place. So, take all the time you need to make a change! Simply communicate your boundaries with your words and follow through with your actions. Here is an example…

If I'm having an argument with someone I love and they begin to speak to me in a way that is hostile or cruel, I can communicate this in a gentle way, "I respect you too much to let you talk to me this way. I will be in the other room when you are ready to talk nicely and respectfully to me." Then simply walk in to the next room. You don't have to yell or scream to communicate this boundary. You simply said what you needed and you followed through with what you said you would do. It is going to take a lot of self-control to not run back and fight it out, but if you are determined to change and set healthy boundaries, you can do this. Over time, the person involved will begin to learn you are serious and in order to talk to you, they must talk in a respectful manner.

Internal Limits

The second set of limits I want to talk about today is internal limits. We need to have a space inside ourselves where we can have a feeling, an impulse, a desire, without acting it out. We need self-control without repression. Which means we may have feelings or attitudes that rise up but we have to have space where we can process without damaging ourselves or those around us. We own our feelings and we own our decisions to "not" act on them. We need to be able to say to ourselves, "No" or "No, not now." Part of spiritual maturity is being able to set personal limits, as in, "No, it's not the time for that" or "I don't need to have that right now."

Romans 14:12 says we will each give an account for the way we lived our lives. This means every dollar spent, every word spoken, every thought thought and every action done will be evaluated and we will have to answer for it. Now I know this can sound pretty intimidating, especially if we are working on things in our own lives, but be encouraged, the Holy Spirit knows how to help you and He knows where the boundaries need to be set, where the limits need to be drawn, and where the "no's" need to be said. You can do this!

CONFESS IT

I declare I am powerful because Christ is powerful and He's residing on the inside of me. God has set up a perfect system for me to thrive. I understand part of His system needs personal boundaries and limitations. I understand I have to use the word "no" in order to say "yes" to the things I really need. I declare I'm going to show up like a grown up. I'm going to set limits on evil and I'm going to raise my standards to respect the person I was created to be. It's time for me to set better boundaries and limits to protect my future and the purposes of God.

I declare this in Jesus' name! Amen

PRAY IT

Jesus, I ask you for Your anointing today! I ask You to anoint my heart to understand what limits You are asking me to make. I understand that I can't always set limits on what I'm around or how people treat me but I ask for your protection and your wisdom to show me what I should and should not allow to be around me. I ask you to give me courage to walk out of the room when I'm not being respected or being treated with care. I ask you to show me if someone is taking advantage of me and to show me a way out. God, I welcome your supernatural activity into my everyday life. Lead me into everlasting life.

I pray this in Jesus' name! Amen.

Doing Some Things well starts with viewing yourself as a whole person and not being afraid of what you might lack. I love the quote: *"He knew what He was getting, when He got you."* This means the God of the universe is not afraid of our humanity but rather died to help us in our humanity to become like Him. It's important to understand that the more you know yourself, the better equipped you will be for the seasons ahead. One of my greatest break-throughs in life was understanding it was my job to know how God created me, what He created me for, and how to most effectively use my personality, gifts, and graces for His kingdom. God does not make clones; He makes each of us with unique personalities, attitudes, interests, and idiosyncrasies. God is a God of the whole person. He's not afraid of our weakness but rather loves us wholly and leads us into wholeness.

One of the greatest misunderstandings many Christ followers have is believing constantly being in need is a bad thing. This is a wrong belief system. God invented needs. God Himself has needs. God created needs for the purpose of getting closer to Him and allowing us to get close to others. It is our immature and broken parts that keep us needing God and draw us to need others. God Himself has a need to be connected, even within the three-part Godhead. The Trinity is a clear example of the connectedness and perfect relationship only God could design. God the Father had a need and asked Jesus to do what He needed to be done. When Jesus was leaving the Earth, after doing what His Father had asked of Him, He also had a need. He requested the Holy Spirit go to Earth and meet this need, and He did. All of these requests were met in the safety of relationship, binding love, and a desire to be connected. Jesus had a need, the Father had a need, and the Holy Spirit had a need, all of them working together in perfect relationship to complete a perfect purpose.

It's important for us to embrace our needs and the needs of others in our process of doing Hard Things. What's even more important is understanding how to meet our internal needs as well. I like to say, *"The more you know yourself, the safer you are."* Having needs keeps us humble and it positions us to know God in a greater way. We were never created to be an island; to perfect ourselves in order to see our needs go away. This was not in the purpose of God. His plan was that we would learn to meet our needs in a healthy way, build unity with others through our need for relationship, while simultaneously walking in an intimate relationship with our Creator. God in His sovereignty made a way to meet our needs at the deepest level.

Today we will look at three different needs we each have and need met. *(Authors Townsend and Cloud have written much on this topic if you desire even greater insight.)*

Bonding

The first need we will look at is the need for BONDING. We all need a constant message that we belong. From the moment our little feet touched this Earth, we should have felt wanted, that we belonged, and that we were home. But some of us never received this experience of bonding. Those who raised us did not provide an atmosphere of love and connection. This fact is extremely heartbreaking. You were born with a need that was never properly met. Yet, there is hope for you. The Bible says that Jesus came for the brokenhearted. He was also sent to tell us that we belong, most of all to Him. So now, as an adult, the Holy Spirit is sending you a message on a daily basis, reminding you that you belong and that you are no longer alone.

For others, we received this message and it was a gift. We all have a need to hear from our Father in Heaven that we belong. We need the eternal voice of our Creator declaring over us, "You belong! There is purpose for your existence!" So, if you have never experienced this relational connection and had these wonderings resolved, this is your first step. You must, with the help of the Holy Spirit, get this basic need met. If not, you will look to fulfill your need to belong in inappropriate and ineffective ways, ultimately realizing that a need met in the wrong way always leaves us wanting.

Separateness

This brings us to our second need: SEPARATENESS. As soon as we are connected and know we totally and irrevocably belong, we need to learn the value of separateness. Though we belong to God, it doesn't mean we are controlled by Him. There is freedom in God's love, without control. Our Father has given us freedom to own our own lives and to lead them as we wish. He lovingly invites us to live close to Him and give our lives to Him wholeheartedly, yet never in a controlling manner. Control is not love but is motivated by fear. The Bible says, "Perfect love casts out fear." If you have a hard time not seeing God in a controlling manner you may struggle with seeing you're self as separate.

Good vs. Bad

Lastly, we have a need to resolve the issue of good and bad. Most of us have a hard time accepting the broken parts of our lives. When we don't see progress in our imperfections, we can hide in perfectionism and secretly hate ourselves. It is always harder to see our strengths as clearly as our weaknesses. While it is appropriate to struggle with the bad things we have done, we must see our sin from God's restorative perspective.

"Children perceive that they are two people - a good person and a bad person. Our need is to resolve that I can live as a good and a bad person in a

good and a bad world and be okay. That's what forgiveness provides. Hiding the bad will appear as 'symptoms'."[6]

This is not permission to give ourselves over to wrong choices or live in sloppy grace. But it does give us permission to accept the things we cannot change and lean on the Lord in our weakness. We should be able to function with joy and peace even if there are broken and immature dimensions in our lives. Joyce Meyer says it well, *"I'm ok and I'm on my way."*

CONFESS IT

I confess I have needs and it is not wrong that I do. I know that You created me with needs and have given me healthy ways to meet them. I choose to not attempt to meet my God-given needs in ungodly ways. I will not easily be sucked into the lie that God does not care; that He has not prepared a place for me. I belong to God! I belong in a family. My father in Heaven is not controlling. He is gracious and kind. I will use my freedom to allow God to fully meet my needs in a healthy way. I am turning over a new chapter and embracing my immaturity and weakness. I am looking to a God who is not afraid of what He got when He got me.

I declare this in Jesus' name! Amen.

---

[6] Townsend

Lord, I understand you made me with needs. I am not bad, though at times I do bad things. You designed these needs for my good, to help me get closer to You and to others. I confess I've not always met my needs in a healthy way. I've given myself permission to meet them in wrong ways or avoid them altogether. Today, I'm taking charge of my needs and wants and I'm embracing them as avenues for connection, love, and fulfillment. I ask You to anoint my heart to know I belong. I belong to You and my needs can and will be met by You. I asked for a deep-seated knowing that I am Yours. I ask You to remind me that You are not a controlling Father but a good and loving Father who operates in freedom and grace. I ask You to help me manage my freedom with diligence and self-control. I pray I would honor You in all of my ways.

I pray this in Jesus' name! Amen.

WEEK FOUR I DO GOOD THINGS

DAY SIXTEEN – *REAPING SUCCESS*

Welcome to week four! We are now getting to the end of our study having covered many vital topics. Our first week was about understanding how Doing Hard Things comes to everyone bringing us real pain. We talked about climbing out of our personal pits by honestly viewing our lives. The second week, we learned about the confidence we can have in knowing we can do all things through Christ who strengthens us. We exposed the weapons of fear and unbelief, reminding ourselves God is bigger than the devil. God sees our faith more than our failure, and He loves to make us a success. Last week, we looked at our own personal limitations and the reality that we all have real needs, limits, yards, and boundaries.

This week, we're going to explore the secrets of spiritual promotion. The Word tells us if we are diligent in Doing Hard Things well, while remaining patient, we will reap a harvest. We can expect a spiritual promotion!

God has created laws we all live by, whether we know it or not. One of His laws is the law of Sowing and Reaping, which is clearly seen in the life of a farmer. When a farmer takes a seed and sows it and then nurtures that seed, he can expect a harvest. This is not a feel-good theology; it's an actual reality we see throughout the Word from the beginning to the end. Eve sowed a seed of disobedience and reaped a harvest of a fallen world. The Israelites sowed unbelief and reaped 40 years of wandering in the desert. John the Baptist sowed unwavering obedience and became a beacon of hope. He was a prophet for the Messiah in his generation. Peter sowed fear and reaped disgrace, but in the second chapter of Acts, he sowed courage and reaped a harvest of revival. The law of sowing and reaping helps us understand how God thinks and it teaches us to be diligent with the things we've been given.

It's not arrogant to expect a harvest if we have sowed good seed. It's called wisdom! When we diligently sow seeds and never look for a harvest, we are not being wise. In Ecclesiastes 3:2, the Bible says there is a season to everything, a season to sow and a season to reap.

So, how do we receive our harvest? The first step in understanding spiritual promotion is having eyes to look for it. A good farmer examines his soil, considers his seed, watches the seasons, evaluates the rainfall, calculates the sunlight, and eventually goes into the field to reap a harvest. Every aspect of this process is vitally important!

"Maturity is looking at our lives as a whole picture and not just partial moments."

Maturity is looking at our lives as a whole picture, not just in partial moments. If we had understood as young men and women that the seeds we sowed would be reaped, we might have been more cautious to sow the right seeds. Some of us have spent decades sowing wrong seed. It may take a long time to weed these areas in our lives. But don't lose hope! We serve a God who holds time in His hands and is able to change things very quickly if we are willing to work hard with Him.

Here's an important exercise we can do today...

Write out all of the kinds of seed you have planted in your life. I understand there may be too many to list, but I want you to try and write down the big ones. It may be that you sowed years of diligence in raising your children. Maybe you sowed years in your education and you want to use it for the Lord. You may have spent time in the Word, memorizing Scripture and declaring it over your life. From every seed you have sown, you can expect a harvest.

Here's one example before you write down yours. Many years ago, I was discouraged with where my life was going. I had given many years to serving the church and loving people. I was tired and worn out and a bit disillusioned by all my years of service. I went to the Lord and asked Him what I should do. You see, I was busy praying, reading the Word, and asking for more change in my life. The Lord spoke this simple word to me and it revolutionized my understanding. He said, "It's time to look for your harvest!" Look for my harvest? I'd never thought of that. I just assumed I was to keep praying harder, worship harder, serve harder and that was my solution.

The picture I received as He spoke was this: I looked up from the ground I had been toiling over to see if my plants had sprung any shoots. When I looked up, I saw a huge orchard full of trees with fruit hanging off of them and I was shocked. At that moment, I understood God was not asking me to sow, or even ask for more, but to expect from Him. I imagined myself walking along and taking the fruit off of these trees that I had worked so hard to grow.

"When we are not willing to reap our harvest our lives stink with rotten fruit."

This is the picture I want to give you. Yes, there are those of us who need to get down on our hands and knees, dig the dirt, water the seed, and make sure that the small shoot is safe. But there are others of us that have been sewing for a long time and it's time to look up and collect our harvest. If I don't collect the harvest, the fruit that is hanging off my tree will fall to the ground and rot. Some of us, because we are not willing to reap our harvest, have areas in our lives that stink with rotten fruit...fruit that others would have absolutely enjoyed if we had been willing to give it to them.

Let's take a moment today and write out the things that you have been sowing for a long time...

If you are new to this reality, it's okay. Write out the simple things you have been doing at this point. I encourage you to make a note so in a year from now, or even years from now, you can look back at this list and expect a harvest.

How Long	Seeds Sown	Expect to Reap
• 5 1/2 Years	• Giving to Missions	• Greater harvest in evangelism in my own community
•	•	•
•	•	•

CONFESS IT

I declare the seeds I have sown will not return void if I take care of them. My life is not and will not be a waste. Every moment I have sowed, prayed, declared, served, and worshiped are moments I will reap a harvest. Lord, You are showing me what season I am in. I trust You!
I declare this in Jesus name! Amen.

PRAY IT

Jesus, I thank you for your law of sowing and reaping. I thank You for creating me not just as one who works the ground, sows the seeds, and never reaps, but as one who can look up and be confident in You...believing You have a harvest for me. I ask You to teach me to expect a harvest in due season. I ask You to help me know what season I'm in and to walk in obedience through the process. Give me a believing heart for the things I've been sowing for years. I'm believing I will reap if I don't faint.
I pray this in Jesus' name! Amen.

DAY SEVENTEEN – *TAKING INITIATIVE*

Turn in your Bibles to **1Samuel 17** and read verses **35-37**...

(We will be hanging out in this story for the next couple of days.)

We've been talking about the secrets of spiritual promotion this week. Not only will we DO HARD THINGS, but we can thrive in the midst of them. Yesterday, we explored sowing and reaping in our lives. We discovered that promotion often comes through the simple act of sowing the right seed to reap the right harvest.

Today, we will look to the Bible's instruction to see one of the greatest characteristics that fruitful leaders possess.

Read verse **35** again and write it below:

_____

_____

_____

_____.

I want you to underline the phrase, "<u>I went out after it</u>." This is a spiritual quality! This quality served David for many years and complemented him as he became the leader of his nation. Leaders go after things. They don't always wait for them to come to them. It's best described in the word Initiative, meaning leading action.[7] It means taking the lead on what needs to be done. David was not cocky or overly confident, he took the initiative. He was simply responding to the HARD THING with confidence.

It doesn't matter what personality you've been given, or what upbringing you may have had, this quality can be nurtured into your present nature. Leaders show up like spiritual grown-ups. If they need change, they look for ways to change, and go after it. They don't need permission to show up.

Years ago, I remember a season of DOING HARD THINGS when the Lord was trying to get me to see my life as an adult. I remember Him saying this phrase to me: "You need to get your power back!" It seemed simple at the time, yet now I seem to use it on a daily basis. What it meant to me was that all the moments in my life when I felt powerless, or that someone was more powerful than I was, were a lie.

God did not create me to live as a powerless person hoping that someone or something would make me powerful. God created each of us to operate with an inner power and His name is the Holy Spirit. The Holy Spirit makes the difference in our lives! When we receive Jesus and the work of the cross, and we invite His Spirit to live within us, we receive power. He is the One who changes our natural to supernatural and gives us the eyes of the Spirit to see what we cannot in the natural. Part of "going after it" in our lives is understanding each of us were created to be powerful beings. Called and anointed to do the work of the Father.

---

7 http://dictionary.reference.com/browse/initiative

Understand the Bible calls each of us leaders. 1 Timothy 4:12 says we are to be an example. Being a leader is being an example. We become a great example when we understand that someone is always looking at us. Simply understanding the Father created us to display His glory. Therefore, we are always teaching the world about Him by our actions. Being a leader is being a model. So, when you talk about leadership in your life, you are confirming what the Bible says: you are an example to your world right now.

The Church has not always gotten this right. They've deemed leadership as those that are on the stage or those operating in a five-fold ministry. These are definitely leaders, operating in a different set of graces, but all of us are called to be leaders in our world. The Church, at times, has sat back and waited for permission to be a leader. God's says, "Don't wait! The time is now! Be the leader you are created to be."

Before we go on, I know you might be asking this question:
What is the difference between godly Initiative and fleshly ambition?

Fleshly Ambition

Fleshly ambition is based on an inner motivation to prove ourselves, to gain acceptance or approval, to avoid rejection, and to maintain control.[8]

Godly initiative, on the other hand, is the fruit of responding to revelation from God related to what He wants us to do, and then doing it in faith.[9]

Godly Initiative

---

[8] www.floydandsally.com

[9] 9www.floydandsally.com

Jesus clearly said He only did what He saw His Father doing (John 5:19). This is very important. When we talk about initiative, we have to have godly initiative, not just fleshly ambition. The difference comes when we commit to only doing what we see the Father doing. For some of us, this will come very naturally because we inherently like to step out. But for others, stopping and waiting to hear what God wants us to do will take incredible self-discipline and diligence. At the end of the day, we want to live lives pleasing to God, so hearing His voice and responding to Him is vital to our spiritual growth.

"Courage is not the absence of fear, but the ability to overcome it."

One last thought: Sometimes, we forget God set up a system to deal with our sin. He says in the Bible that if we have pride, the next thing that happens is a fall (see Proverbs 16:18). Sometimes, as believers, we get so caught up in trying to have the right motives, we miss the opportunity to simply "do something." Part of maturity is knowing that if our motives are not right, God will deal with it. We cannot be afraid to fail but rather must be prepared to step out anyway in the midst of fear and understand that God can take whatever we've been given to sow and make it beautiful.

CONFESS IT

I confess I am a person who takes initiative! I am not going to sit back and wait until I can do things perfectly, but I am going to listen to my Father's voice and respond immediately. I am a leader! And part of the leadership I'm called to is taking the lead when others do not. I'm going to "go after it" until I get it! I will not be afraid of failure but I will trust God and His sovereign grace to help me in the process. I will not wait for permission to be obedient or to get what is rightfully mine. I will show up like a spiritual grown-up! If my Father says stop, I will stop. If He says go, I will go. I declare this in Jesus' name! Amen.

PRAY IT

Lord, I confess I have not always taken the initiative when You asked me to. I am beginning to understand what You are asking of me. I want to be like a David! When the enemy comes, I go after him and defeat him. I want to be one who does not wait for someone else to step out or invite me into the process, but I want to be a leader who sees what's ahead and runs to it. Forgive me for being apathetic at times and not responding. Forgive me for running ahead of You and not waiting. Teach me today to follow hard after You and give me a right spirit within me. I pray this in Jesus' name! Amen.

DAY EIGHTEEN – CELEBRATE SUCCESS

Leaders learn to celebrate small victories, gaining confidence for bigger ones!

Turn back to **1 Samuel 17** and read **35 - 37** again.

Write verse **36** below:

_____

_____

_____

_____

Here, we see David acknowledging and celebrating his prior successes. He says, "Your servant has killed both the lion and the bear." He's saying, "Listen, I've done this before! I've been doing this, and I will do this!" His history of success helped him believe that, with God's help, David would do it again. It's the same with us. Our history of success in God keeps us believing we will do it again.

Building a history in God is one of the greatest ways to build confidence in Him. If we have gone through defeat and we've made it, we don't fear defeat like we once did. If we have success and acknowledge and celebrate it, we build confidence that success will come again. The more we acknowledge the process and embrace our progress, the more we will expect the same outcome.

I have been in ministry for 17 years. I have had high times and low times and a bunch of stuff in between. One of my favorite things to do right after leaving a speaking event, whether it felt like a success or not, is to say to my family, "Let's celebrate our victories and ignore our losses." I simply mean: we need to remember we obeyed God and did what He asked us to do. That, in itself, is a victory! We need to protect ourselves from the enemy beating us up over our defeats and celebrate the fact we actually did what God asked us to do.

God also asks us to not despise the days of small beginnings. I believe at times we can be so focused on large defeats or large victories, we forget to acknowledge our little successes. We have a "fairytale" experience where we believe our BIG victory will catapult us into success in every area. But this is not always how the kingdom of God works. Even David had to fight a lion and a bear before he took on Goliath, and so will we. We have to get really good at working on our history with God!

So, my questions for today are:

What are the bears and lions in your life right now?

_____

_____

_____

_____

_____

Are you doing them well? Or are you allowing yourself to be defeated by looking at the "Goliath" in your life?

_____

_____

_____

_____

Are you doing them well? Or are you allowing yourself to be defeated by looking at the Goliath in your life?

_____

_____

_____

_____

CONFESS IT

Lord, I confess I will celebrate my small victories! I understand my small acts of obedience, faith, and love prepare me for greater things. I'm building confidence in You, God! You have not brought me this far to leave me and I'm trusting in the reality that You are preparing me for my Goliath. I declare I'm celebrating my victories and ignoring my losses on a daily basis. I understand my history in You is vital to my confidence in You. I will embrace the small things and prepare for the larger things!

I declare this in Jesus' name! Amen.

PRAY IT

Lord, I ask You to help me today! I understand I have been caught up expecting greater success in the larger things of my life and not always believing the smaller victories matter. I ask You to anoint my heart to celebrate the moments when I obeyed You, whether big or small. I ask You to give me eyes to see my lion and my bear. They will help prepare me for my Goliath. I pray for grace to do Your will! I pray for faith to see what I presently cannot!

I pray this in Jesus' name! Amen.

DAY NINETEEN – *EXPECT SUCCESS*

Leaders don't always get success but they should always expect it!

Lets go back again the story of David and Goliath. Turn back in your Bibles to 1 Samuel 17 and read 35-37 again; write verse 37 below:

_____

_____

_____

_____ .

Secrets To Success

David gives us a few secrets to DOING HARD THINGS that led to His success!

#1   The first thing we see about David is that his faith was in the Lord. His first phrase says it all, "The Lord who..." It's important to understand the Lord is the One who leads us and gives us success. He is the author of fulfilled promises. He understands our need for greatness because He put it there. Once David understood it was the Lord who was helping him, his faith grew. He understood the greatness of God, placed upon his small frame and personal gifts, allowed him to expect victory. David's faith grew so big it overpowered his fear. We talked a lot about this in Week Two but until our fear is overcome by our faith, we will see little spiritual promotion. Doing HARD THINGS well must begin with, "The Lord who..." if we are to see success at all.

#2

Secondly, we find when David is attacked, he doesn't just let the enemy come after him and then scare him away. David turns to go after him to kill him. Some of us get caught in allowing the enemy to continue to pick on us and provoke us. We will only deal with him when we've had enough. This is not what a leader does! A leader doesn't wait to be picked on over and over again, before finally rising up and dealing with it. But rather, a leader goes after it immediately. Understanding what's at stake. David understood if the lion or the bear ate one of his sheep, they would come back in a stronger confidence to take more sheep. David didn't just chase the bear or the lion off, he went after them, and killed them. This is a great spiritual principle! The next time the devil comes after you, don't let him hang out. Get up and fight him with the Word of God and shut him up. We can't expect victory if we're not willing to fight with complete abandon and commitment.

#3

Thirdly, we see David used this phrase, "The Lord who rescued me... Will rescue me!" David is saying, "If He did it then, He'll do it again!" This should be our mantra as Christ followers.

I want you to say this 10 times out loud...

"If He did it, He'll do it again!"

Our expectation in Christ creates faith! Faith pleases God and creates evidence. David's faith in God (his history in Him) allowed him to expect victory. When David spoke the words, "God would do it again," I would suggest God responded. The Bible says God responds to faith! (see Luke 17:5) How do we know that David's expectation rested in the Lord? Because the Bible says it. Turn to Psalms 62:5. Please write it down here ...

_____

_____

_____

_____.

I love how the Message Bible states it.

"God, the one and only —
I'll wait as long as He says.
Everything I hope for comes from Him,
so why not?"

I love this thought. Why not expect? Why not hope? Why not believe for success? David did and so can you. So, today, ask yourself this question:

Do I really believe God gave me success in the past? And if so when? _

_____

_____

_____

_____

_____.

What can He do again in my life?_____

_____

_____.

Remember, no one can believe for you! No one can expect God like you can. God responds to your faith. As we have looked today at the characteristics of a leader who expects victory, I want to encourage you with this thought: The Lord who has done it, will do it again. He loves to get us out of pits to walk in freedom and thrive!

CONFESS IT

I declare God is helping me to DO HARD THINGS well! I understand He is leading me to my success and helping me to grow my faith. Spiritual promotion is coming my way because I'm doing the Hard Things well. I understand that the enemy would love to pick on me and provoke me. I will not allow it! When he comes, I'm coming after him as well. So watch out enemy! I'm not playing games any longer. I will deal with you quickly and swiftly under the power of God. I am confident the God, who has rescued, redeemed, delivered, and set me free, will do it again!

I declare this in Jesus name! Amen.

PRAY IT

God, I ask You for grace today to do Your will. I understand part of the secret to my success is understanding that You are a God who has and will do what He promised. I ask You to give me faith to lean into your consistent love and faith in me. I ask You to give me eyes to see the enemy who comes to kill, steal from, and destroy me. I ask You to empower me to not just hinder his attacks but to go after him and destroy him with the Word of God. I ask that as I lean into You, my faith would be stronger than my fear and that I would be one that says, "My God will do it again!"

I pray this in Jesus' name! Amen.

DAY TWENTY – COMMISSIONING

We made it! This is our last day together. I hope you have learned much in this process of Doing Hard Things and I trust you've grown in confidence. The fact that you have been willing to go through this study and lean into God during this season will reap great benefits. He sees it all! It all counts!

Today, we will conclude with our story of David and Goliath. Let's look at our last characteristic of Doing Hard Things well, which leads to spiritual promotion. Please review 1 Samuel 17 and read 35-37 again.

I want us to take note that we can't have or expect a victory if we don't have it germinating inside us. If we have an unbelieving heart, a critical spirit, or we are overwhelmed with self-pity, we can't expect God to respond. If you do the work on the inside, you will see it on the outside. The Bible says, "You yourselves are our letter, written on our hearts, known and read by everyone."

When David communicated he could kill this Philistine, I would suggest that those around him saw a faith they couldn't deny. They hadn't seen any other warrior with such confidence. They saw David's supernatural faith because once they heard this, they believed and immediately began to prepare him, even though he was not a trained warrior.

I believe this exact thing happens to each of us! When we begin to really believe the God who did it before will do it again, others will see what we have been building on the inside. And once they see our strong faith and confidence in God, they will mirror that same faith and confidence as well.

Our whole study has been about understanding you are anointed to do Hard Things well! You may not have realized, but you are growing in such a way that others will be able to see a change in you. They have been watching you do your Hard Things and have grown in courage to do their own. They will grow in confidence as they watch you respond to the Holy Spirit and determine to have faith. They will find their own personal limitations and boundaries as they watch you operate and manage your own yard well. They will see you define your life by your faith and not just your failure. They will watch you believe your God is bigger than the enemy and his weapons of fear and unbelief will not hinder you. They will take hope in your diligence to sow seeds and look for a harvest. They will watch a person who believes God, takes incredible initiative, and declares the God who has done it, will do it again!

Growing up, I had many learning disabilities. Just the fact that each of you are holding this book is an incredible miracle. I could never have written or published a book on my own but it was the grace of God and the supernatural power of the Holy Spirit enabling me to do what I could not do on my own. At the age of 17, the Holy Spirit got ahold of my life and began to challenge me to believe for greater things. What the world had said over me was not the truth: that I would never be able to read and write in a strong way.

So, I started small and began to write and share teachings. When I felt defeated, I would go after those lies and destroy them with the Word of God. I did not allow the devil to lie to me for very long.

As the years went by, victories would come and so would defeats. Yet, I continued to expect success because I had seen it before.

Years later, I had a dream to write a study that would help many people. The study was called "Keep Calm and Finish Strong." This study was my Goliath. It was the biggest battle I had ever faced. Each day, as I sat down to write, it took everything I had. It did not come naturally for me. It was not easy. It was excruciatingly hard. But, like a hiker who climbs a great mountain, I held onto my backpack and put one foot in front of the other. On the day the book was complete, I felt a huge triumph in my heart. I had killed my Goliath!!! I've had learned to DO HARD THINGS.

And now, as we finish I Do Hard Things, I'm struck with the reality that the God who did it before, has done it again...and He will do the same in your life. This is not the end of the story. You have bigger mountains to climb and greater heights to conquer. There are many people waiting for you on the other side of your obedience as you climb out of your pit of pain and into your promised land.

CONFESS IT

I declare I Do Hard Things well! I am no longer sitting in a pit of pain but I've climbed out and I'm on my way to the next mountain. I understand the God, who created me and loves me, is working it all out for my good. I declare every truth I have learned in the Word and in this study will take root in my life and will not return void. I confess I will help others as they face Hard Things, and I will teach them what I've learned about You. I believe You who have done it before, will do it again. You will always be there to help me!
I declare this in Jesus name! Amen.

PRAY IT

Lord, thank You for loving and leading me on this path of freedom and wholeness. I thank You that Your hand has been upon me throughout these four weeks leading me and guiding me into perfect truth. I thank You that You revealed areas of my heart where I was stuck, sitting in a pit of pain, and not knowing the way out. I thank You that I can do all things through You and that You're strengthening me today. Thank You for revealing to me my own personal limitations and the godly boundaries that need to be in place. I ask You to make me the person of initiative You've called me to be. I will celebrate my small victories and believe for greater victories up ahead. Anoint my heart at this moment to receive all You have prepared for me.
I pray this in Jesus name! Amen.

Made in the USA
San Bernardino, CA
01 March 2017